PIUS XII AND THE HOLOCAUST

Pius XII and the Holocaust

A Reader

A *Catholic League Publication*

Catholic League for Religious and Civil Rights
Milwaukee, Wisconsin

ISBN: 0 - 945775 - 01 - 6

Catholic League for Religious and Civil Rights
1100 West Wells Street
Milwaukee, Wisconsin 53233

Dedication

To the memory
of the millions
of Christians and Jews
who were victims
of the Holocaust.

Contents

Preface

Preface

As I write these words, Christians and Jews are quietly marking the fiftieth anniversary of *Kristallnacht,* re-garded by many as the opening scene in the tragedy we have come to call the Holocaust.

We, both Christians and Jews, cannot reverse the course of time and undo the horror of those dark days which saw the senseless destruction of millions of human beings. But we can learn many lessons from the record of that tragic period of history.

The Holocaust was a shared horror in which millions of Christians and Jews perished. And while it was truly a shared calamity, we must acknowledge that although not all the victims were Jews, all the Jews were indeed its victims.

The past can be a great teacher for those of us who are willing to take the time to seek out the truths which it hides and the lessons that are there to be learned. This small book attempts to manifest some of those truths with particular regard to one man who has been much maligned by those who would choose to make him a scapegoat for the failings of nations and diplomats and countless others who through indifference or inaction saw the Holocaust loosed on the world.

The two authors we have chosen to help set the record straight are men of impeccable credentials and eminently qualified to serve as our guides in this study. Father Robert A. Graham, S.J. is a scholar in the fields of international affairs and Vatican history. The late Dr. Joseph L. Lichten was a Polish diplomat who experienced first-hand the brutal destruction of his homeland and the senseless killing of his Jewish brothers and sisters.

As Dr. Lichten so eloquently puts it, "It is our sacred duty to establish what happened — what was not done but also what was done, not merely for the sake of consolation but in order to understand the truth and to do justice to those who stretched a helping hand to Jews in those tragic days."

Pope Pius XII stretched out a helping hand. That gesture of compassion and love was followed by countless others.

Rev. Virgil C. Blum, S.J.,
President and Founder,
Catholic League
for Religious and Civil Rights.

November 10, 1988
the 50th Anniversary
of *Kristallnacht.*

HOW
TO
MANUFACTURE
A
LEGEND

Rev. Robert A. Graham, S.J. is a scholar and writer of distinction in the fields of international affairs and Vatican history. A former editor of *America* magazine, Father Graham has written numerous articles and several books, his best known being *Vatican Diplomacy.* He writes a regular column on the Vatican for *Columbia* magazine. His past 17 years have been devoted to the monumental task of editing an 11-volume series containing the documents of the Vatican Secretariat of State during World War II.

How to Manufacture a Legend:

The Controversy over the Alleged "Silence" of Pope Pius XII in World War II.

By Robert A. Graham, S.J.

During World War II (1939-1945) Pope Pius XII lent a strong hand in support of the harassed Jews of Europe. The Vatican was one of the few remaining points of assistance left on the Axis-controlled continent. Increasingly, with the evidence of their own experience, local and world Jewish representatives learned to turn to the pope for help. This confidence was never disappointed. Uninfluenced by anti-Semitic propaganda or over-awed by the ruthless Axis power visible on all sides, the Vatican, that is, Pius XII, intervened on behalf of Jews, individuals and groups, at strategic moments. This action it took either on its own initiative or following representations coming to it from numerous Jewish rescue organizations keeping vigilance over the unfolding drama. Such assistance was not sporadic or incidental or perfunctory but consistent — and persistent. It was not the accidental product of some curious circumstance, but the result of policy and principle. And the local Jewish leadership, with the world Jewish organizations, recognized this with gratitude. For as the war progressed, it was clear that in a continent writhing in suffering, Jews were easily among the most imperilled.

The full truth of what was happening would become known only later. But enough was known to produce, on the Vatican's side, innumerable interventions with governments still susceptible to admonitions. At the death of Pius XII, Jewish spokesmen, who knew the record, came forward with tributes to the late pontiff's services in the name of humanity, for the victims of the Holocaust.

At this point commences a stupefying paradox. The general assistance of the Vatican to Jews during World War II is fully documented, with chapter and verse, in the archives of both the Vatican and the Jewish organizations, such as the World Jewish Congress and the American Jewish Committee, not to speak of the official U.S. War Refugee Board. How does it come about that, in later years, the wind changes abruptly and violently? The Pope is found violently criticized by those who a short time earlier had been effusive in praise. For it was not until 1963, five years after the Pope was in his grave, that the past was, so to speak, itself buried in silence, as if inconvenient. In the spring of that year, in Berlin, a theatrical piece written by a hitherto unknown young German playwright roused enormous polemics inside and outside of Germany. The debate is continuing, a quarter of a century later.

Had something new been discovered? Had some secret aspect of the war years come to light hitherto unknown? Nothing of the sort. But a new climate had developed which put the issue in a new psychological rather than historical perspective. The calendar may help us to discover what happened and, in the process, to improve our understanding of the curious controversy over the alleged "silence" of Pius XII.

The above-mentioned play, called "The Deputy" (*Der Stellvertreter*), by Rolf Hochhuth, was staged in February 1963, barely a few months after the close of the first session of the epoch-making Second Vatican Council. As is well known, this historic assembly of all the Catholic bishops, called by Pope John XXIII, aroused unprecedented interest in world opinion. Within the Catholic body politic the council opened entrancing perspectives, particularly the relations of the Catholic Church to other Christians — and to Jews. Ecumenism was on the march, after repeated false starts.

There were other relevant events at this time. U.S. public opinion was increasingly disturbed by the mounting moral challenge opened by the Vietnam war. The spectacles of lives and money consumed in a conflict seemingly without object raised profound moral scruples, not to say guilt complexes. Finally, shortly before, the trial of Adolf Eichmann in Israel brought out, as never previously, the destruction of European Jewry in all its somber and tragic colors. Is it too much to suggest that perhaps, considering this junction of disparate circumstances, the figure of the Pope emerged as a sort of substitute, or surrogate, of the conscience of us all? The hypothesis is unprovable, but it helps to explain why the Hochhuth play triggered a controversy that is still going on, quite beyond the literary merits of "The Deputy."

Whatever its origins, a psychological transformation does not justify distortion of the historical reality. Facts remain facts and are not to be relegated to insignificance as if they did not happen. Yet this is what is happening: all that the Pope did for the Jews, and also all that the Jews said in praise of Pius XII, has been covered with a curtain of oblivion. The real silence has been the silence of polemicists who have succeeded in closing one eye to the reality, thereby leading the public into a grotesque conception of the role of Pius XII in World War II.

The language itself has suffered from this misinformation. Playwright Rolf Hochhuth criticized the pontiff for his (alleged) silence, but even he admitted that, on the level of action, Pius XII generously aided the Jews to the best of his ability. Today, after a quarter-century of the arbitrary and one-sided presentation offered the public, the word "silence" has taken on a much wider connotation. It stands also for "indifference," "apathy," "inaction," and, implicitly, for anti-Semitism.

The image presented today is that of a Pope immobilized in the face of atrocities. Hence the self-revealing question, "Why did not the Pope *do* something?" Or, tendentious allusions to the "inaction" of the Vatican, as if the only action conceivable is that of making public and provocative statements regardless of their real and possibly disastrous and pernicious consequences for the Jews themselves. This is to cancel out too easily the factual record of the continuing real assistance of the Vatican to European Jewry, of which the appropriate documents and declarations of those concerned are convincing (but suppressed) witness.

It may surprise the contemporary generation to learn that the local Jewish communities, and the world Jewish bodies did not, for the most part, urge the Pope to "speak out." Their objective was far more concrete and down-to-earth. They invoked the real or supposed influence of the Holy See on governments in respect to certain situations arising at one or other points of the tragedy. Appeals to world opinion, high-sounding though they may appear, would have seemed cheap and trivial gestures to those engaged in rescue work. (There were many Allied propagandistic appeals, and threats, which had no effect and possibly hastened action by the Eichmann crew.) The crying need in those years was for effective pressure on persecuting governments, pressure that often enough could only be exercised by discreet and even roundabout methods.

The need to refrain from provocative public statements at such delicate moments was fully recognized in Jewish circles. It was in fact the basic rule of all those agencies in wartime Europe who felt keenly the duty to do all that was possible for the victims of Nazi atrocities and in particular for the Jews in proximate danger of deportation to "an unknown destination." In Geneva at this time, for instance, the World Council of Churches found itself obliged to refrain from any public statements about Nazi a-trocities, on the grounds that this would bring to nought whatever real good they were presently accomplishing. Yet, behind the scenes, without fanfare, the Council, under the Secretary General Visser 't Hooft, deployed, like the Vatican, effective assistance to the Jews.

The drama faced by the International Committee of the Red Cross, with its seat likewise in Geneva, is perhaps even more striking. The Committee is officially charged by international agreement with supervising the application of the Red Cross Conventions on Prisoners of War. But the needs of civilian internees (read, "Jews") increasingly alarmed the members of the committee. The Red Cross had no real knowledge of the extermination camps at this time (in the autumn of 1942) but the harshness of German procedures, and even more so the sinister disappearance of so many thousands into the maw of deportation, suggested the necessity of an open and public protest on the part of the Committee. With profound regret, the Geneva Red Cross decided that a public protest, a) would have no effect, b) would compromise what real good the Committee was already doing for the internees, without benefit of public declarations. And indeed in the following war years, the International Committee of the Red Cross was able to achieve a great deal in its efforts at alleviating suffering.

There is no one who today questions the reasonableness of the "silence" of the World Council of Churches, or of the Committee. But the same factors were operative in like manner for the Vatican: no good would be accomplished by public protests, and on the contrary, what good was yet possible would be compromised by provocations. In his own reaction to the negative decision of the Red Cross, the Geneva representative of the World Jewish Congress, Gerhart Riegner, accepted its validity. If something could yet be done to save the threatened Jews, then this should be followed up, in place of a protest: "I believe — he (Carl Burckhardt) told the Committee representative — a protest is necessary only in the case where there is really nothing more to be done at the time. But if one can still exercise some influence and if one wishes to refrain from a protest, it is necessary to *act* and not to satisfy oneself with passively recording news of deportees." Riegner's stand, preferring action to words, is in contrast with the contemporary prevailing obsession with "open protests," as if they were an end in themselves.

The Vatican, too, had to face the possibility — even the probability — that its own direct protests against the deportation of Jews would undermine the slender basis it had already for effective interventions. Any one who pretends to pass moral judgment on the actions of persons and institutions during the stress of

World War II owes it to the truth to consider adequately the real margin left for action. This courtesy, or justice, has demonstrably not been extended to Pius XII. The result has been the construction of images totally out of relation to reality. It is significant that the argumentation against Pius XII is uniformly of a negative nature: the Pope did not do "enough." He did not say "enough." This open-ended approach can be applied, at will, to almost any other institution of personality, and it reeks with subjectivity and arbitrariness. Under such a formula of "enough," nobody is immune from criticism.

Even the word "silence" is relative. Pius XII was not "silent" during World War II. He was not even "neutral." In this the Holy See differed from the above-mentioned World Council of Churches and the International Committee of the Red Cross, which found themselves unable to make any statements, even the most generic, protesting Nazi atrocities. The Pope's public statements, from his first inaugural encyclical of October 1939, were clearly directed against the National Socialist regime, and were so understood on both sides.

It is true that the papal language, in these circumstances, was indirect, round-about and imprecise. But there was no doubt, for those who cared to read, as to what he meant. Take, for instance the Papal discourse of June 2, 1943. Pius XII first assured his listeners that he regarded all peoples with equal good will. "But" — he went on — "do not be surprised, Venerable Brothers and beloved sons, if our soul reacts with particular emotion and pressing concern to the prayers of those who turn to us with anxious pleading eyes, in travail because of their nationality or their race, before greater catastrophes and ever more acute and serious sorrows, and destined sometimes, even without fault of their own, to exterminating constraints."

The Pope went on to say that the rulers of nations (that is, the Nazis) should not forget that they could not dispose of the life and death of men at their will. Such words, despite their indirectness and circumlocution carried a message we should be able to understand and appreciate today. They are fully confirmed in the record, as we know it.

A year later, on June 2, 1944, the Pope returned to this theme. The tone of concern is obvious: "To one sole goal our thoughts are turned, night and day: how it may be possible to abolish such acute suffering, coming to the relief of all, without distinction of nationality or race." This is not "indifference," or "apathy" or "inaction."

It is sometimes said that Pius XII should have been more "prophetic" during World War II. If what is really meant is that he should have excommunicated Hitler and be done with it, the proposal is anything but "prophetic." Such an idea could emanate only from someone with an outmoded, simplistic concept of the role of the papacy, drawn from some overblown literary tradition. But, in the real sense, Pius XII, standing in the heart of the Axis world when Britain stood alone and the United States was far away and frozen in isolationism, did exercise a real prophetic mission with his inspiring discourses to a world disoriented and dispirited by the apparent triumph of evil. For a world hungry for guidance Pius XII was far from "silent" or lacking in the prophetic quality.

A great injustice has been done to the memory of Pope Pius XII. An even greater wound has been administered to history. The controversy over the wartime role of the Pope is riddled with misrepresentations and falsehoods, expressed too often in bitter tones that surprise and disappoint those who perhaps mistakenly believed an era of *détente* and a mutual desire for understanding had arisen. We have been witnessing a staggering disregard and a bland, unembarrassed disavowal of formal statements of those in the best position to know the facts. In the process a mountain of fantasy has been created, without any real foundation in the record.

Sooner or later, the facts will assert their rights. With time, the wheel will come full circle and return to the point from which it departed in 1963. This was the time when in his lifetime as well as after his death Pius XII was recognized by the most authoritative spokesmen for what he was in reality, one of the best friends the Jews had, in one of the most tragically dark days of the long, long history of the Jewish people.

PIUS XII's
DEFENSE OF JEWS
AND OTHERS:
1944-45

Rev. Robert A. Graham, S.J., the author of the preceding article, is also the author of the following monograph which was first published by the Catholic League in 1987. The introduction (which begins on page 32) was written by the late Dr. Joseph L. Lichten, author of *A Question of Judgment: Pius XII and the Jews,* which comprises the third section of this present book.

PIUS XII'S DEFENSE OF JEWS AND OTHERS: 1944-45

by Robert A. Graham S.J.

with an Introduction by Dr. Joseph L. Lichten

Ever since Rolf Hochhuth's *The Deputy* made its appearance in 1963, it has been an unshakable axiom of popular mythology that Pope Pius XII was, if not actually a crypto-Nazi, at least guilty of criminal cowardice and insensitivity in the face of the Holocaust. It is accepted as a truism that the Pope's failure to act or even to speak out against the atrocities of the Nazis made him a silent partner in the massacre of millions. In the hands of some writers, this alleged collaboration of the Pope is adduced as evidence of the anti-Semitic and pro-fascist nature of the Catholic Church as a whole.

The Deputy was more than merely a play. It was a sustained exercise in character assassination that was resoundingly echoed in the popular press. The production of that play coincided closely with the publication of Anne Frank's *Diary* and the trial and execution of Adolf Eichmann. The world needed to give vent to its horror, and with no more real Nazis left to punish, the image of a pusillanimous pope offered just the right scapegoat.

So *New York Times* columnists write about the "unctuous silence" of Pope Pius XII. Specialists in Holocaust studies characterize the Pope as a symbol of moral irresponsibility. The Bronx Museum of Art displays a painting called "Nazi Butchers," featuring Pius XII in full papal regalia. A certain species of hat-in-hand Catholic writers beat their breasts loudly over the cowardly silence of the Vatican, as if this proves their own liberality of mind. And an ABC News correspondent, covering Pope John Paul II's visit to Munich, remarks that this city was the cradle of Hitler's Nazi movement, knowing the allusion will not be lost on a public that has been taught to view the papacy as a pawn of the Third Reich.

Pius XII is beyond harm. He received his final reward a generation ago, and before he died he had the consolation of receiving the gratitude of worldwide Jewry for his noble efforts on their behalf. Yet while his detractors can no longer injure him, their slanders and insinuations continue to plague the Church, for when a pope is defamed, the Church suffers.

Unfortunately, when these cheap accusations began to surface, when they were stealing into popular consciousness and shaping public attitudes, the historical data needed to refute them were not at hand. For more than 15 years, Father Robert Graham, the distinguished Jesuit historian and former editor of *America* magazine, has been editing the Vatican archives from this tragic period. His work proves beyond any reasonable doubt that in its diplomacy and in its direct humanitarian works, the Holy See was a champion of peace, of compassion and of human dignity in the midst of the most terrible passion and violence.

The present booklet is but a brief summary of the contents of Volume X of the *Acts and Documents of the Holy See Relative to World War II*. It relates the humanitarian efforts undertaken by the Vatican, under the personal direction of Pius XII, during the last stages of the war to alleviate suffering and to protect human life and human rights. It is a record no Catholic need be ashamed of. Before and after Hitler's seizure of power, the Catholic Church in Germany was a formidable opponent of Nazism - so much that Hermann Goering complained in 1935 that "Catholic believers carry away but one impression from attendance at divine services and that is that the Catholic Church rejects the institutions of the Nationalist State. How could it be otherwise when they are continuously engaging in polemics on political questions or events in their sermons ... hardly a Sunday passes but that they abuse the so-called religious atmosphere of the divine service in order to read pastoral letters on purely political subjects." And the Church was persecuted for these "abuses." Catholic lay leaders were murdered. Catholic organizations and schools were suppressed. Priests and nuns were framed on false charges and thrown into concentration camps.

In 1937, when the leaders of the Western democracies were scurrying to Munich to negotiate with Hitler, the Holy See condemned the theory and practice of the "Nationalist State" in the encyclical *Mit brennender Sorge*.

When Jews felt the cruel sting of Nazi hatred, the German bishops protested, "Whoever wears a human face owns rights which no power on earth is permitted to take away,"echoing Pius XI's declaration, "We are all spiritual Semites."

Pius XII had just ascended to the Chair of Peter when the world was engulfed in war, and that war provided a cover for the ultimate Nazi atrocity; the deliberate genocide of an entire people.

This called for action, not words, and it was with action that the Holy See responded. While Britain and the United States were refusing to admit refugees to their territories, the Holy See was distributing thousands of false documents — life-saving passports to freedom — to the beleaguered Jews. While the Allies were trying to use the rumors of death camps for war propaganda, Catholic priests, nuns and laypeople were hiding Jews in their flight to safety, and often paying for it with their lives. While the Allied military leaders were refusing to bomb the rail lines into camps, Vatican diplomats were dealing with the leaders of occupied areas, trying to keep Jews off the trains.

Some have accused the Church of taking an interest only in baptized Jews, and it is true that Church spokesmen were able to make a more persuasive case to the Nazis to save the lives of Jewish Catholics. But as Father Graham shows so clearly, the fatherly concern of the Holy See extended to all the victims of war, regardless of race or creed.

In one tragic instance, the Archbishop of Utrecht was warned by the Nazis not to protest the deportation of Dutch Jews. He spoke out anyway and in retaliation the Catholic Jews of Holland were sent to their death. One of them was the Carmelite philosopher and mystic, Edith Stein.

It could be asked whether these good works were enough, whether it would have been better for the Pope to have de-nounced from the rooftops the crimes that were occurring. This thought troubled Pius XII, and he confided afterward to an associate, "No doubt a protest would have gained me the praise and respect of the civilized world, but it would have submitted the poor Jews to an even worse persecution."

With the benefit of historical hindsight, one may question this judgment and many others. One can suggest that a mistake was made here or there, that sometimes caution got the better of courage, that more lives might have been saved if the Pope or his agents had acted differently. But these things will never really be known.

What cannot be questioned is the integrity, the charity, and the deep commitment to humanity of Pius XII. It is idle to speculate about what more he could have done, for unlike most of the leaders of his day, he did very much.

INTRODUCTION

by Dr. Joseph L. Lichten

In the fall of 1963 I was granted an audience with His Holiness Pope Paul VI, who thanked me for a book I had presented to him as a token of my esteem. Since the book dealt with the events of the Second World War, the conversation turned quite naturally to Pope Pius XII. I lamented that the full record of the Holy See's wartime activities during the most trying period for the world Jewish communities could not be fully known until the Vatican archives were opened. Pope Paul smiled warmly and said: "I hope I will be able to be of help in this."

The archives were indeed opened, undoubtedly for reasons more crucial than my own comment, and three years later I received Volume I of the *Actes et Documents du Saint Siege Relatifs a la Seconde Guerre Mondiale,* autographed by Paul VI, dated May 26, 1966. Ten bulky volumes of the *Actes* have since appeared, and recently Father Robert Graham, S.J., has written a remarkable synthesis of the documents contained in Volume X, which covers the last 18 months of the war.

Father Graham's monograph, which concerns the humanitarian interventions of the Holy See, pictures the period of the war so full of tragic memories, interspersed with only a few more hopeful moments.

It was the time when Polish Jewry, three and half million strong, with a thousand-year tradition of organized communal life and renowned scholarly record, ceased to exist; it was the time when Jews from other European countries were being annihilated in Nazi concentration camps and gas chambers. Hungary, due to its unusual internal political situation, was the only country in which a majority of the Jews managed to survive, living however in constant fear of what the next day would bring.

Naturally, the tenth volume of the *Actes* can be fully understood and appreciated only in conjunction with the events of the previous years, described in the earlier volumes, and Father Graham in his monograph used such a retrospective method. He provides, for example, sights into the peregrinations of the children evacuated from Romania to Palestine, across Bulgaria and Tur-key, in which the Apostolic Nuncio Andrea Cassulo played an influential role. Through the year 1944, Pope Pius XII provided funds to aid Romanian Jews, especially those in Transnistria. Similarly, every rescue action in Slovakia in the closing year of the war was being undertaken in the spirit of the Pope's personal message to the Slovak government, opposing the deportation of Jews to death camps. Even so, only a quarter of the Jewish community in Slovakia survived. Although the outcome was tragic, the Holy See's interventions should not be minimized. Father Graham cautiously assesses the circumstances:

> Obviously, one should not suppose that whatever positive results were achieved through these initiatives were due solely, or even largely, to reputed Vatican 'influence.' To do so would be to underestimate the vast and intensive activity of the Jewish organizations them-

selves. Yet, the gratitude of the Jewish leaders, such as Rabbi Safran, was no less sincere and justified.

In Hungary, there were still 750,000 Jews at the beginning of 1944. Their "dark hour" began in March of that year, immediately after the German invasion of the country. Writes Eugene Levai in his classical book on the martyrdom of the Hungarian Jewry:

> From that day on, acting in accordance with the instructions of the Holy See and always in the name of Pius XII, the Nuncio never ceased from intervening against the disposition concerning Jews, and the inhuman character of the anti-Jewish Legislation.

Most impressive in that respect was the open telegram which Pius XII sent on June 25, 1944 to the Hungarian leader, Admiral Horthy. The text of the wire in included in the volume, and Father Graham extensively quotes from it.

The documents in the *Actes* also described in detail the Holy See's activities in Italy, paying special attention to the well-known involvement of Church institutions in hiding Jews in Rome. Much of this information has now become part of an official record. (In fact, I devoted several pages to this subject in my own monograph, *A Question of Judgment: Pius XII and the Jews.*) Father Graham includes in his volume many letters of appreciation from several Jewish organizations and prominent Jewish community leaders. He also notes that in some cases there was "synchronization of papal and Jewish rescue action." Volume X, he says, "provides more graphic substance to these acknowledgements in the precise narration." A watchful student of the mounting literature on this subject will undoubtedly notice that in studies critical of the Holy See's behavior these facts are somewhat bashfully shunned; they seem to upset some writers' applecarts. The new volume brings these facts back to light.

Another issue which merits additional clarification is whether, as some authors have asserted, the Holy See acted more often and more vigorously in behalf of baptized Jews than in behalf of Jewish communities. Father Graham considers this question in his monograph and concludes that the nuncio's efforts to save converted Jews did not detract from their action in defense of the haunted Jews - actions which became ever more energetic as time went on and the danger of total annihilation drew nearer. Furthermore, their pleas for the baptized were as natural as was the anxiety of the Jewish institutions over the fate of their own co-religionists. Finally, there was an element of naivete' on the part of those who alleged that papal nuncios engaged in preferential treatment of baptized Jews, because a countless number of baptismal certificates were not genuine. When a Red Cross worker objected, saying that forged documents violated the Geneva Convention, the Apostolic Nuncio in Hungary replied:

> My son, you need have no qualms of conscience because rescuing innocent men and women is a virtue. Continue your work for the glory of God.

It is beyond the scope of this brief introduction to analyze the Holy See's efforts against the background of Allied assistance - or lack of assistance - to European Jews in distress. There was a dead silence over the matter for a very long time. Only recently was the "terrible secret" of Western complacency revealed; only in the past few years have people begun to ask why Auschwitz was not bombed.

Father Graham's monograph will stimulate many more reflections.

The closing months of the war sealed the fate of world Jewry, marking a disaster, the extent of which cannot be fully assessed even today, almost 40 years later. If we are to have a balanced view of the past, it is pertinent that we should know as many facts, as many details as is possible. It is our sacred duty to establish what happened - what was not done but also what was done. It is especially important that we should know what was done, not merely for the sake of consolation but in order to understand the truth and to do justice to those who stretched a helping hand to the Jews in those tragic days. Many authors have been in a hurry to write, to accuse, to blame. Perhaps it would have been wiser to wait for the last volumes of the *Actes* to appear.

Humanitarian Intervention

To provide a documentary basis for the scientific study of the Holy See's actions and policies during the Second World War, the lat Holy Father Pope Paul VI, authorized publications of the pertinent papers of the Secretariat of State of His Holiness Pope Pius XII. The decision to publish those confidential papers was without precedent. The papers have been edited by a group of Jesuit historians of several nationalities. The first volume, entitled "The Holy See and the War in Europe, March 1939-August 1940," was published in 1965. Other volumes followed, and now volume 10, "The Holy See and the Victims of the War, January 1944-July 1945," is presented to the general and the scholarly public. It concerns the humanitarian interventions of the Holy See in behalf of a wide variety of the war's victims, both civilian and military, during the final year and a half of the Second World War. In this volume, the term "humanitarian intervention" is intended to exclude other forms of papal intervention or action, for example, on the diplomatic or pastoral planes. The distinction between such categories is of course not always clear, but the differences are sufficient in most instances to justify publication of the *Actes* in different volumes which, though covering the same chronological period, deal with significantly different classifications of action.

The final year and a half of World War II was the most destructive era in the history of the West. Intransigence and ruthlessness were at their peak as the destructive hours approached. In this conflict of giants, individuals or groups counted for little. "Military necessity" was the first rule, transcending all other considerations. The victims were myriad: wounded soldiers, prisoners of war, civilians subjected to bombardments, individuals taken as hostages or threatened with death reprisals for actions deemed unlawful by a local commander, and whole populations facing starvation. Some of these evils and hardships are "classic" and are witnessed in any war. But the deportation of countless thousands to an "unknown destination" on racial grounds alone was a new atrocity of whose existence the documents published in this volume give ample evidence. Many of those same documents also record the efforts of the Holy See to help Jewish communities in the German sphere of occupation. Many of them document the extraordinarily close cooperation and understanding existing between the Holy See and the many Jewish organizations dedicated to the welfare and safety of their co-religionists. Even before the beginning of 1944, the world Jewish organizations had recognized in the Holy See a friend who was willing — and often able — to help in the many situations heavy with tragedy developing in occupied Europe. Through the documents, the synchronization of papal and Jewish action clearly emerges. The concerns of the Jewish organizations were also those of the Holy See. Sometimes, the Holy See acted directly on the appeal of a Jewish organization, well informed as they were on the condition of their own people. At other times, the Holy See acted on the basis of reports received from its own representatives on the scene — in Bratislava, Buch-arest, Budapest, Berlin, and elsewhere. The papal represen-tatives were obviously on close terms of confidence with leaders of the local Jewish communities from whom they received timely indications of imminent dangers to the Jews of that particular country. In many instances, the Holy See had already acted upon information received from its own nuncios when appeals from Jewish organizations, themselves informed with some delay, arrived at the Vatican.

Public Acknowledgement

This relationship of confidence based on earlier performances is, of course, known in its general outlines. After the war, the Jewish organizations themselves publicly acknowledged the sympathy and cooperation they received from the Holy See. Volume 10, however, provides more graphic substance to these acknowledgements in the precise narration, day by day, month by month, of the Holy See's correspondence with the most active international Jewish organizations. Among the more important of these are the Emergency Committee to Save the Jewish People of Europe, the World Jewish Congress, the American Jewish Congress, Agudas Israel World Organization, Vaad Hahatzala of the Union of Orthodox Rabbis of the United States and Canada, *Hijefs* (Schweizerischer Hilfsverein fur Judische Fluchling im Ausland), the Jewish Agency for Palestine and the American Jewish Committee. In 1944, the War Refugee Board came into existence and represented, in fact, the united effort of the various American Jewish organizations. During and after the war, the War Refugee Board publicly acknowledged its close relationship with the Holy See, as well as the services rendered to the cause by the Holy See. The documentation also includes correspondence from eminent rabbinical leaders who made special appeals to the Holy See; among them are the Grand Rabbi of Jerusalem, Dr. Isaac Herzog, the Grand Rabbi of the British Empire, Dr. Joseph Hertz, and Rabbi Abraham Kalmanowitz, leader of the rabbinical school of Mir, in Lithuania.

Military and Political Situation

The military and political situations during the last year and a half of the war should be briefly recalled. This was the time of the german occupation of Rome (second phase), the slow Allied advance from Anzio, and the bombing of Montecassino. The closing months saw the war front advancing on the cities of Northern Italy, threatening these seats of earlier culture with utter destruction. Hostages were often shot in reprisal for acts of resistance to the occupation. The number of prisoners of war falling into the Allied hands multiplied, and in Germany, hundreds of thousands of Italians stood without protection as "military internees." The formula of "unconditional surrender" proclaimed by the Allies was met with "total mobilization" in the Reich along with stern repression of all signs of "defeatism." As the war drew to its climax, neither side felt constrained to consider the victims. The iron law of war left little room for the work of any would-be Good Samaritans. The Holy See, however, refused to reconcile itself to this inhumane atmosphere, and it continued to insist on its humanitarian role, despite misunderstanding, failures, and even opposition.

The work of the Vatican Information Office was a visible sign of the Holy Father's paternal solicitude for all victims of war, notwithstanding their nationality, political opinion, race or religion. It consisted of transmitting the names of persons taken prisoner or interned. In many cases, this was the first information received by anxious families about loved ones known to be in the theater of war. Previous volumes in this series discuss the importance attached by Pius XII to this service, one of the few ways in which he could publicly demonstrate his humanitarian concern.

Vatican Information Office

The Vatican Information Office struggled for years to gain recognition and cooperation. In fact, the German government never did consent to the Office's initiatives. When combat ended in North Africa, thousands of Axis prisoners were in Allied hands, but in the spring of 1944 it was still impossible for the Vatican representatives to transmit the names by radio from Algiers to the Vatican. In the United States, similar difficulties prevented radio transmissions of lists of prisoners and internees. As late as June 14, 1944, the Apostolic Delegate in Washington explained that "security reasons" put the matter beyond discussion. On March 18, the Secretariat of State submitted a verbal note to the British legation at the Vatican regretting the delays and obstacles encountered in securing radio transmission of short messages from Algiers. The American authorities were apparently favorable, but not the British, for as that message stated, "Msgr. Carroll gives his assurance that the American authorities have kindly granted their consent to these radio communications of messages regarding civilians and prisoners according to short sentences agreed upon by common consent. The British authorities, on the other hand, have not given theirs." In the end, before the tide of the war advanced and the prisoners were moved, the lists and messages had to be forwarded by way of Spain after long delays.

Italian Military Internees
in Germany

In 1944, a new aspect of the Pope's concern for prisoners of war arose in response to the plight of Italian soldiers who had been brought to Germany after the Armistice in September of 1943. Their condition received scant attention in the world press, but they constituted a new category of "war's victims." They were not regarded as prisoners of war but as "military internees"; that is, they had no recognized rights under the Geneva Red Cross Conventions. The Allies refused to permit passage of material assistance destined for them, because the distribution was not under Red Cross supervision. And in the last year of the war, when supplies were short in Germany even for civilians, what help could they expect from local resources, even supposing good intentions on the part of their captors?

On December 23, 1943, Cardinal Maglione, the Pope's secretary of state, had formally asked German Ambassador Ernst von Weizsacker if the Reich government would permit Vatican assistance to the Italian internees. No answer was ever given. In the meantime, innumerable inquiries and appeals from distraught relatives in Italy were forwarded by the Vatican to the nuncio in Berlin. The nuncio reported to his superiors that the foreign ministry told him to apply to the special office for interned military set up by the Republic Fascist embassy — whose government, of course, the Holy See had not recognized. Nuncio Orsenigo asked if he might not, despite the non-recognition and in view of the desperate situation, approach this office. In fact, Msgr. Orsenigo was able to visit camps or labor battalions where Italians were detained, especially in the vicinity of Berlin.

Even the repatriation of those seriously handicapped and unfit for any war purpose encountered agonizing difficulties. One of the charitable projects to which the Nuncio Orsenigo devoted himself was the return of Italy of those badly in need of medical attention, especially victims of tuberculosis and malaria. On February 7, 1944, Cardinal Maglione wrote the nuncio: "The Holy Father, in his charitable and ardent solicitude to relieve the sufferings of those sons of his and bring some consolation to the families, so sorely tried in their dearest affections, is firmly resolved to try every possible way to obtain that Italian soldiers interned in Germany should be treated humanely, and that those in precarious conditions of health should be repatriated promptly."

Orsenigo said he then appealed on general humanitarian grounds, without getting any answer except that the internees had the Italian Republican Fascists to help them and that they received letters and packages from home. In the meantime, repatriation encountered further difficulties. On April 13, 1944, Orsenigo said he heard that some repatriated "volunteers" had simply deserted and gone into hiding once they found themselves in Italy. On May 19, the nuncio happily informed the Vatican that the first transport of disabled men had left for Italy. But on September 7, the nuncio reported to his regret that the German government had "completely suspended" the repatriations - to avoid the hostile comments, he was told, cause by the distressing condition of these unfortunates. No more sick or wounded would be allowed to leave Germany.

"The consequences of these measures," reported Orsenigo, "are disastrous and cruel; in the camp infirmaries languish numerous seriously ill persons who call out for their families."

'Free Workers'

In the meantime, as a result of an agreement between Mussolini and Hitler, the internees were transformed, in theory at least, into "free workers." But this was to be a slow process which remained true only for those in good health. Orsenigo reported on September 15 that he had protested to the Foreign Ministry against the suspension of the repatriation of the sick.

In these months the Holy See used not only the channels of Berlin, Berne and Rome but also the Nunciature of Vichy and Father Biasio Marbotto, who was located in Poland, where Italian internees were also detained. The French Relief Agency, under Abbe Jean Rodhain, was able to print prayer books in Italian and to distribute them to the relatively few Italians in the so-called "mixed camps," but the French had no access to the main camps. On November 14, 1944, as the second winter approached for the Italian internees, the Secretariat of State renewed his urgent appeal to the German government. The note, addressed to Ambassador von Weizsacker, referred to the still-unanswered note of December 22, 1943. It acknowledged that, despite the lack of response, it had been able "in certain cases" to provide religious assistance in camps where Italian internees were held, and also to contribute some medicines and concentrated foods. The letter also cited the condition of French internees and the dangers that were said to menace prisoners and internees of certain races or nationalities (a reference to the treatment of Jews). Could not the German government, asked the Holy See, gratify world opinion by releasing the sick, the aged, women and children and arranging for their repatriation, while at the same time issuing a statement guaranteeing humane treatment for prisoners and internees of whatever race or nationality?

There followed, in this note, the Holy See's statement of its own hopes and ambitions:

> The Holy See which, carrying out its universal mission of charity, has left no stone unturned in order to relieve in some way the unspeakable sufferings of so many human beings in the course of this international conflict, once more addresses the German Embassy, begging it to be so kind as to submit to its government the considerations set forth above, in the hope that measures dictated by human and Christian piety, which in any case, would be to the advantage of the German people itself, will be taken and carried out, in favor of prisoners and internees.

Rome, 'Open City'

In the beginning of 1944, Rome had been under German control for nearly four months. More than six months were yet to pass before German troops withdrew from the city in retreat to the north. By January, the city had become the hiding place of thousands of persons who were eluding the occupation power or the Fascist Republicans. Swollen by refugees drawn by what they though was the protection of the "Open City," Rome experienced great problems of food supply. So while the Holy See was trying (always in vain) to get some assurance that Rome would be demilitarized and spared from bombing, it was also concerned with averting starvation.

On the night of February 3, the Republican (neo-Fascist) police broke into the extra-territorial Basilica of St. Paul's Outside-the-Walls and brought to light that the entire monastery was a shelter for the very people the neo-Fascists were seeking: military officers, Jews, ex-members of the dissolved Carabinieri (military police) and various young persons avoiding military service with the Fascist Republicans. Some were dressed in clerical garb. It was no great secret that the many ecclesiastical homes in Rome — and not just those enjoying extraterritorial status - hid people of various categories whose safety was threatened. In the Roman Seminary at St. John Lateran there was hidden nearly the entire National Committee of Liberation - only a few paces from the headquarters of the Gestapo Police Chief Kappler on the Via Tasso. They were never molested. An invisible protecting hand poised over them.

The thoughts of the Holy See on the subject of asylum were revealed in a notation by Cardinal Maglione following a conversation with the German ambassador. On January 6, 1944, His Eminence recorded that Weizsacker had complained about the existence of fugitives in religious houses, whose presence had been revealed by nighttime raids. This situation, said the ambassador, diminishes his authority with his superiors, and he complained to the cardinal about such infractions of the German occupation laws. What did the Cardinal Secretary of State reply to the charge of such "irregularities"? He told the ambassador that he had himself urged the religious houses to be "correct" and "prudent," but he added that he hoped they would not be judged too severely. Later, he wrote down this summary of his sentiments expressed to the German envoy:

> It is difficult to accuse a priest or a member of the faithful of having been unfaithful to his duty because out of pity, he has given food to an escaped prisoner or even a German deserter. If, on our side, we recommend prudence and correct behavior, comprehension should be shown also on the German side for acts of human pity such as the ones mentioned above. And since mention was made of laws, I pointed out that the latter are applied excessively and with too great severity: at the front and behind the front populations of several thousands of persons (women, children and old people) are forced to abandon their homes in a few hours, in some cases a few minutes ... and then everything is destroyed (household goods, houses, fields ...). Sufferings are increasing to an unspeakable extent.

The Cardinal, hinting at the change of fortune that comes to those who take up the sword, wrote that he had hoped the Holy See would not be put in a position of being unable to say a good word for Germany in the future.

Following the September Armistice, the doors of convents in Rome had been opened to all categories of refugees, regardless of their politics, religion or race. This unusual situation was already under study when the raid on St. Paul's provoked a new examination. Some of the reports then submitted to the Secretariat of State of His Holiness help illuminate the situation. For example, Msgr. Robert Ronca, rector of the Roman Seminary, reported on February 6 that he had 56 "guests." He said they had all signed a statement not to compromise the neutrality of the Holy See and the State of Vatican City and also not to perform any political activities (at least not on the premises; the National Committee met elsewhere). DeGasperi, he added, did not sign the document as he was about to leave the Lateran anyway. (He moved to comparable shelter as the guest of Cardinal Celso Costantini at the Propaganda Fide. None of the guests wore clerical garb, and all used their real names, said Msgr. Ronca.

A similar situation was reported for the Vatican City itself. In a February 13 report, Msgr. Anichini, the rector of the Canonica of St. Peter's, said his guests were living in crowded quarters and that they comprised military men, students, foreigners, Jews, displaced families and others. "All together," he said, "there are about 50 individuals in serious danger of being arrested and shot or deported. Those less exposed to risks have already departed of their own free will; the others prefer to face all dangers in the Canonica in the shadow of the house of the Father to whom they address the anguished invocation: 'Salva nos perimus'."

A third report came from a pontifical institute which was not in Vatican City but which also was not extra-territorial. There, according to the rector, Msgr. Erminio Vigano, in early March were to be found 52 persons including many Jews. Such had been the situation, he said, since the previous October. After the October 16 raid on the ghetto of Rome, Jews had sought and found shelter in many religious houses. The largest group had gathered in the convent of the Sisters of Notre Dame de Sion on the Gianicolo. There, for months on end, lived about 200 Jewish men and women. Despite the conspicuous crowding and the inevitable complaints, the convent was not molested.

Feeding Rome

The problem of feeding the Roman population as military operations came closer to the Eternal City occupied the Pope's thoughts in the latter days of the German occupation. On February 26, the Holy Father's close personal friend, Enrico Galeazzi, and Father Pancrazio Pfeiffer were invited to Marshall Kesselring's headquarters on Monte Soracte, where they discussed the question of supplies for Rome with General Westphal, the German chief of staff. As far as supplies were concerned, they told the German official, the situation of Vatican City could not be separated from the situation of Rome itself. The two visitors were assured that the German military commander was cognizant of the Romans' need for food. But General Westphal complained of the indifference and passivity of the local population. "The general," the papal aides reported, "announced somewhat emphatically that if the citizens of Rome continued to fail to collaborate with the German authorities to ease these difficulties, the marshall intends to withdraw his protection from the city, as regards food." In fact, however, Vatican trucks were allowed to proceed to the North to collect food supplies.

In further concern for feeding Rome, the Vatican proposed the creation of a "Vatican flotilla," which would have consisted of about 20 small coastal vessels which would have plied between Ostia or Civita Vecchia and northern ports, bringing supplies. The plan never materialized, however, because the Germans delayed their approval and later, when the Allies were in Rome, they, too, rejected the proposal.

The Vatican's efforts to assure a stable food supply for the citizens of Rome were further hampered by an unreliable communications system. For example, between June 4, 1944, when the Allies entered Rome, and the following October, no courier bags were permitted to leave or enter the Vatican, so, for more than four months, the Vatican was effectively cut off from the rest of the world. The only regular contact possible during this interval was through Vatican Radio. In the meantime, diplomatic reports and other messages essential to the conduct of Church affairs piled up in Madrid, Lisbon or Berne, awaiting clearance from Allied authorities. The only exceptions to the embargo occurred when military personnel with authorization to leave or enter Rome unofficially brought letters with them. The Holy See did not protest the communications blockade, hoping no doubt that the problems would soon be alleviated. Instead, they continued for months.

Via Rasella and the Fosse Ardeatine

The idea of "Rome, the open city," was dear to the heart of Pius XII, and he devoted most of his energy during 1944 to making that ideal a reality. The Holy Father's sentiments were shared by most Romans and even by the leasers of the Resistance. Accordingly, most members of the Resistance avoided provocative acts that might evoke drastic reactions, thus jeopardizing the existing uneasy equilibrium. Nevertheless, a few members of the Resistance thought it dishonorable that in Rome alone, of all Italian cities, there should be no "rising," no open sign of anti-Fascist resistance. The most active of such groups was the communist-directed GAP (Gruppi Azione Patriotica) which, after a series of minor attacks, decided that the time had come for a major gesture. On March 23, 1944, in the Via Rasella, a bomb exploded as a German unit was marching by. It killed 33 soldiers.

Regarding the action as a direct challenge to its authority, the German High Command in Berlin ordered the immediate execution of 10 Italians for every soldier who had been killed. According to the order, issued in Hitler's name, the reprisal must be completed within 24 hours. What followed, of course, is well known. By noon the next day, a convoy bearing the victims of the reprisal, who were yet unaware of their impending fate, was directed to the Ardeatine caves on the outskirts of Rome. Under the direction of SS Lt. Col. Herbert Kappler, 335 Italians who had no connection with the Rasella affair were taken from various prisons and shot to death in groups of five and buried in the caves. The executions were carried out in secrecy, but on the next day German authorities briefly announced that 10 Italians had been executed for every soldier who had been killed in the Via Rasella. Months passed, however, before the identities of all the victims became known.

The only record of the incident to be found in the archives of the Secretariat of State of His Holiness was a memo written by a Vatican secretary reporting a call received at 10:15 a.m. on March 24. The caller, who described the bombing, added: "Countermeasures are still not known; it is thought, however, that for every German killed, 10 Italians will be executed."

Beyond a doubt, the bloody massacre of German soldiers in a Roman street, with its obvious provocative intentions, prompted considerable concern and alarm in the Vatican. The prospect of a German reaction threatened to disrupt whatever tranquility remained in the city. It is impossible to suppose that Pius XII could fail to react with some effort to avert the worst, and the record of the Pontiff's concern for the lives of the unfortunates who fell into German and neo-Fascist hands during those months shows eloquently his sensitivity to such situations.

In the absence of documentation, therefore, one is left to surmise that the Pontiff intervened personally, as he had on so many earlier occasions, through his nephew Prince Carlo Pacelli or through the General Superior of the Salvatorian Fathers, Father Pancrazio Pfeiffer. Nor should one be surprised that such a supposed intervention had little chance of success; the order had come from Berlin and, moreover, what argument could a papal emissary use in favor of restraint? For the past several months, the Pope had argued that German restraint would ease the tension in Rome. Suddenly, the entire papal strategy had been undermined by the spectacular and tragic liquidation of 33 German soldiers.

Ironically, about 35 of the Ardeatine victims had already been the objects of papal intervention. The Pope had intervened on behalf of many captured resistance leaders, including Bruno Buozzi, Giacomo Matei, Leon Ginzburg, Giuseppe LoPresti, Enzo Malatesta, Gianfranco Mastei, General Angelo Oddone, Mario Sbardella, Carlo Scalara, Stefano Siglienti and Antonello Trombadori.

Trombadori, who was chief of the GAP in Rome, managed to convince his interrogators that he had "never got involved in politics," thanks no doubt at least in part to the favorable testimony given by the Secretariat of State. Such manifest readiness by the Holy See to intervene for the lives of members of the Resistance strongly indicates that on March 23 and 24 the Holy Father also used all his influence in the direction of restraint, after calculated "resistance" on the Via Rasella.

The German embassy to the Vatican withdrew into discreet silence, and on March 29, von Weizsacker's office said that inquiries about persons jailed by the Germans should be addressed to the German police command, Via Tasso, 155, the notorious headquarters of SS Lt. Col. Herbert Kappler, the Nazi chief of police in Rome.

The Cities of North Italy

After June, 1944, threats to Rome were alleviated by the shift of the war front to North Italy. But the shift created a new concern: the safety of cities famous for their art treasures, cities such as Florence, Ravenna, Bologna and a hundred smaller towns in the line of battle. At this time, too, Allied artillery was trained on the industrialized cities and the ports of the North: Turin and Milan, Venice and Genoa. From these heavily populated areas, appeals came to the Pope, imploring his intervention to avert disaster.

It is true that the Allies had given assurances that artistic monuments would be respected. Experts on Italian art and architectural treasures had conducted serious studies, identifying targets to be treated with deference. But the experience of Montecassino showed that military commanders on the spot could easily disregard the recommendations of their own art-specialists-in-uniform. Therefore, such assurances as that made by the British minister on May 13, 1944, were not greeted with much elation or confidence. Minister Sir d'Arcy Osborne, in a note to the Vatican, said: "The Holy See may therefore rest assured that, in so far as the use of Allied air and ground forces are concerned, every possible precaution is being taken to preserve Italian historic and artistic monuments from the effects of military operations."

From the German side, the mood to spare such cities as Florence appeared more than positive. On June 1, the German embassy told the Vatican that Florence had been declared an "open city."

Siena was to be treated in the same manner, with German troops to be routed around the center of the city. The Secretariat of State was pleased to communicate the German declaration to the American charge, Harold H. Tittmann, Jr., and to the British minister, Sir d'Arcy Osborne. And on June 20, it sent a more formal note to the two Allied diplomatic missions, as well as to the German embassy and to the nuncio in Berlin, in which it expressed the earnest prayer that the "incomparable" towns of Tuscany, such as Florence, Pisa, Siena, Lucca and Arezzo, not become theaters of war. On June 29, Msgr. Tardini noted that Nuncio Orsenigo's reply came from Berlin, citing the Foreign Ministry, caused him to suspect that German plans for safeguarding Florence and other towns only concealed a strategy for disengaging the Germans militarily. In fact, Orsenigo informed his superiors that the Germans wanted the Allies to wait from six to 18 hours before entering the cities abandoned by the German forces. "Who knows, on the contrary," recorded the worried and suspicious Tardini, "that they don't have the diabolical plan to bring about (or at least to provoke) their destruction?"

In the meantime, reports on the sufferings of the civilian population in the path of war came to the Vatican in increasing numbers. On July 15 — via the nuncio in Switzerland, by wireless - the Cardinal Archbishop of Bologna, Giovanni, Battista Nasalli Roc-ca di Corneliano, supported an appeal from the mayor of that city. Noting that Bologna had been bombarded 15 times, with 1,600 victims and 3,000 factories destroyed, he asked that Bologna be declared an open city; he affirmed that Marshall Kesselring was favorable.

Bologna, of course, was an industrialized city, which made it an ideal target for Allied bombing. Assisi, however, was not, so the Holy See could write with more confidence on behalf of the city of St. Francis. It was gratified to receive the Allied diplomats' assurance that "no permanent headquarters or other installation which can justify bombing by our enemies will be established there."

On August 2, the Secretariat of State sent to the German embassy an appeal from the Archbishop of Siena, Msgr. Mario Tacabelli, urging that the Germans declare Siena a "city of hospitality." On August 9, a similar note went to the British legation on behalf of Bologna as an "open city." The official military reply was that the Commander in Chief "cannot enter into any undertakings, such as declaring cities to be 'open,' which might prejudice the success of his operations and so lead to unnecessary loss of life among the troops for whom he is responsible." On October 21, the Secretariat of State informed the Allied di-plomats that, according to information from the Cardinal Arch-bishop of Bologna, all preparations had been made to make Bologna a "city of hospitality."

Milan, also heavily bombarded, appealed through the Vatican to the Allies for special consideration. On October 24, the Secretariat of State transmitted to the British legation an appeal that at least the center of the city, in which the Duomo and a large hospital were located, be spared. "The Secretariat of State of His Holiness," said the note, "cannot but make its own the request of the Cardinal Archbishop of Milan, and trusts that the Allied commanders will not fail to adopt in good time all possible preventive measures in order that such a famous monument and the lives of so many innocent people may be spared." The Allied reply was, of course, noncommittal. "Every precaution" would be taken, consistent with military operations.

In the closing months of 1944, the Secretariat of State sought special consideration for Venice, Imola and Verona, with a similar lack of results. The Germans said Venice could not be declared a "city of hospitality" because it was in the was zone. Finally, in response to a request that the Vatican intercede on behalf of the city of Vercelli, Msgr. Tardini explained how useless such appeals were — "that the requests of the Holy See that certain places not become battlefields have received only vague and unreassuring replies.."

The Action of the Holy See
for the Jews of Europe:
Romania

B y 1944, as the end of the war approached, the Vatican was thoroughly aware of the Nazis' ruthlessness and in-transigence, especially toward the Jews. The evaluation of Msgr. Domenico Tardini, secretary of the Congregation for Extraordinary Ecclesiastical Affairs, is typical. On August 7, the papal official transmitted to the German ambassador an Allied appeal on behalf of foreigners or stateless persons, mostly Jews, located in camps in Northern Italy. At the requests of the American and British governments, the Holy See asked the German government to permit them to be gathered and sent to a port on the Adriatic coast, from which Allied ships would transport them to Southern Italy or Africa. The proposal, which emanated particularly from Myron C. Taylor, was issued just a few weeks after the July 20 attack on Hitler's life. According to Tardini, the Allied refugee specialists believed that, under the existing circumstances, the Nazis might be disposed to a concession, an act of clemency. Tardini himself did not think so. After handing the proposal to von Weizsacker, he recorded: "I told him I thought otherwise. The Nazis will get worse, the worse things are going for them." Nevertheless, telegrams in support of the project, as unrealistic as it may have been - went to the papal representatives in Berlin and Berne.

Still, there was a chance to provide some help to the threatened Jewish communities in the Balkans. This, then, was the scene of an intensive "war of telegrams" during 1944 in Romania, Slovakia and Hungary. The Apostolic Nuncio in Bucharest, the Romanian capital, was Msgr. Andreas Cassulo, who had previously secured relief for the Jews deported to Transnistria, a new Romanian province annexed from the Soviet Union in 1941 which had become a veritable penal colony. The nuncio's relations with the Jewish community, and especially with the Chief Rabbi, Dr. Alexander Safran, were close and confident. On January 22, 1944, Cassulo reported to his superiors the latest preoccupations of the Romanian Jews and the role that the Holy See might play. The time seemed opportune to secure the withdrawal of all Jews in Transnistria back to the center of the country, which was known as "the Kingdom." If they remained where they were, they would be in danger of falling into the hands of the retreating Germans. It was also proposed that the many orphans in this group might be sent to Palestine.

Not waiting for instructions, the nuncio immediately began diplomatic maneuvers, asking the government to raise the age limit of the orphans from 12 to 16, thereby increasing the number eligible for the exodus to Palestine. Soon after, the Grand Rabbi of Jerusalem asked the Holy See to intervene in a similar manner, but having already acted, the nuncio pointed out that further Vatican action would be superfluous. In a March 16 report to the Vatican, he said the government seemed ready for conciliation and that it would do even more were it not afraid of the reaction of the country's anti-Semites. The nuncio informed the Vatican that the civilian administration of Transnistria had been dismantled and that the population, including the Jews, "will be evacuated this side of the Nistra," that is, to safety beyond the reach of the Germans.

As for the orphans, on July 11, the nuncio informed Rome that the first Romanian refugee ship had arrived in Istanbul carrying 250 children from Costanza. Other ships would bring more refugees, he said, "and in this way the difficult question, which gave us so much work in the past, is reaching a successful solution." Naturally, he said, the gratitude of the Jewish community in Romania is felt deeply. Rabbi Herzog of Palestine also sent his thanks to the nuncio.

Obviously, one should not suppose that whatever positive results were gained through these initiatives were due solely, or even largely, to any reputed Vatican "influence." To do so would be to underestimate the vast and intensive activity of the Jewish organizations themselves. Yet the gratitude of the Jewish leaders, such as Rabbi Safran, was no less sincere and justified.

The Holy See's support was also sought in another, less efficacious attempt to evacuate Jews from Romania to Palestine. The Jewish organizations had secured the services of a Turkish vessel, the *Tari,* to shuttle refugees between Costanza and Istanbul-Haifa. The International Red Cross, however, insisted that the ship first obtain a guarantee of safe passage from the Germans. The Vatican instructed Nuncio Orsenigo to solicit the Foreign Ministry for such a guarantee. Unfortunately, though, at that same time, the Germans learned that the Turks, responding to Allied pressure, had refused to deliver chromium to the Reich, so the *Tari* was not allowed to sale. Notwithstanding Turkish policy, it is doubtful in any case that Berlin would have conceded safe passage to the *Tari.*

Deported to Auschwitz

Among the first people to be deported to Auschwitz in May and June of 1944 was a group of Romanians whose fate is often identified with the tragedy of the Jews of Hungary. In the Arbitration of Vienna (August, 1940) the northern part of Transylvania (known as Siebenburgen, Ardeal or Erdely) had been transferred to Hungary, with dire consequences for the 150,000 Jews there. Following their deportation, Rabbi Safran, in a June 30 letter, informed the nuncio of their relatives. Other Jews in Bucharest expressed similar feelings to the nuncio and to the Vatican itself. Months later, on December 11, they reported that little information was yet available about the fate of the deportees. Some, it was said, had been exterminated at Auschwitz; others had been sent to labor camps. No one had been able to penetrate the cloud of mystery hovering over their destiny. Jewish leaders asked the Holy See to seek Berlin's permission to distribute packages of medicine and clothing, and as late as January 31, 1945, the president of the International Red Cross declared his organization's willingness to cooperate with the Holy See in aiding the Jews of Transylvania, who had been missing since mid-1944. As a result, the nuncio in Germany was instructed to explore ways of providing assistance.

The relationship of trust and confidence between Nuncio Cassulo and Chief Rabbi Safran is amply demonstrated by several communications. On May 25, 1945, the nuncio transmitted to his superiors two unqualified tributes. Rabbi Safran, he informed the Vatican, "has expressed to me several times ... his gratitude for what has been done for him and for the Jewish community. Now he has begged me to convey to the Holy Father his feelings of thankfulness for the generous aid granted to prisoners in concentration camps on the occasion of the Christmas festivities. At the same time, he told me he had written to Jerusalem, to the Chief Rabbi (Herzog), and also elsewhere, in America, to point out what the Nunciature has done for them in the time of the present difficulties."

Rabbi Herzog's February 28 letter to the nuncio contained these expressions: "The people of Israel will never forget what His Holiness and his illustrious delegates, inspired by the eternal principles of religion which form the very foundations of true civilization, are doing for us unfortunate brothers and sisters in the most tragic hour of our history, which is living proof of divine Providence in this world."

After the armistice of August 23, 1944, Rabbi Safran publicly reiterated the same sentiments which the intervening months had given no cause for him to revise. To the entire international Jewish community, on December 3, 1944, he declared: "My permanent contact with, and spiritual closeness to, His Excellency the Apostolic Nuncio, the Doyen of the Diplomatic Corps of Bucharest, were decisive for the fate of my poor community. In the house of this high prelate, before his good heart, I shed my burning tears as the distressed father of my community, which was hovering feverishly between life and death."

The Action of the Holy See
for the Jews of Europe:
Slovakia

In the spring of 1944, after long months of apparent standstill, a new alarm was sounded for the surviving Jewish population in Slovakia. But the storm did not really break until September, when an ill-fated and perhaps premature "rising" prompted the Germans to assume control of the country, with the Jews as the major scapegoat. The initial alarm of a renewed deportation of jews came from the World Jewish Congress in the United States. On January 29, 1944, it warned the apostolic delegate in Washington, D.C., Archbishop Amleto Cicognani, that a census of Jews was being taken, with a view toward deportation. The Nuncio Rotta in neighboring Hungary issued a similar warning at that same time. As alarming as those reports were, they did not, in fact, signal an immediate deportation. The charge' Burzio reported that there was no immediate danger to the Jews, and subsequent events proved him right. On February 25, the Secretariat of State passed on to Burzio a warning by the United States that it would take into account the treatment accorded to the Jews in Slovakia, and that it would hold President Tiso and his collaborators responsible for any mistreatment. That same spring, two young Slovaks escaped from Auschwitz, bringing to their people the facts of the deportees' destiny. On May 22, the papal charge' Burzio sent to the Vatican the famous Auschwitz Protocol written by the two young escapees. However, that report did not reach the Vatican until October, due to the blockade of Vatican communications after the liberation of Rome in June, 1944.

Message to Bratislava

After the abortive rising of September, the Jews were brought back to the camp at Sered, from which they were deported. Their destination, however, was not Auschwitz, which was being dismantled in the face of the Red Army advance, but camps in Germany itself, notably Bergen-Belsen. Alerted by Burzio, Roncalli and others, the Holy See sent instructions on September 19 to the charge' in Bratislava, directing him to intervene for the Jews in the name of the Holy See, first to the Slovak foreign ministry and then to President Tiso. According to his instructions, the charge' was to point out "that the Holy See expects from the Slovak authority an attitude in conformity with the Catholic principles and sentiments of the people of Slovakia." It added that a collective action by the bishops might also prove useful. On the following day, the Holy See dispatched a verbal note to Karol Sidor, the Slovak minister to the Vatican. "The Holy See," declared the note, "moved by those sentiments of humanity and Christian charity that always inspire its work in favor of the suffering, without distinction to parties, nationalities or races, cannot remain indifferent to such appeals...."

Two weeks later, the Slovak minister told the Vatican that the Germans had indeed intended to deport the Jews, but that, through the personal protest of President Tiso, on the grounds of the Slovak constitution, the Jews would not be deported but only assembled in labor camps. It was a German promise, as Dr. Tiso later recognized, that was not kept.

As had happened so many times before, the action of the Holy See, informed by its own envoys, anticipated the urgent appeals that soon flooded into the Vatican from Jewish spokesman around the world. On September 23, Myron C. Taylor of the War Refugee Board in Washington apprised the Secretariat of State of the situation in Slovakia, and Rabbi Herzog in Palestine sent a similar message two days later. On September 28, Msgr. Tardini informed the U.S. representative that the Holy See "has already hastened to intervene with the aforesaid government, in order that the feared measures may not be applied." He added that the assistance of the Slovak episcopate had also been solicited. In an October 6 telegram, the charge' Burzio reported that the arrests in Bratislava which he had anticipated had begun on September 29. On that same day, he said, he went to President Tiso to use his intervention at least for the baptized Jews, who were very numerous. Burzio confirmed that the government had declared the Jews had the protection of the laws and that the government "would not consent to their deportation."

By October 26, however, Burzio reported that the deportations had already begun and the search for Jews in hiding was continuing without foreseeable relief. His report had a profound impact in the Vatican, which had been following simultaneous events in Hungary. Msgr. Tardini — who was now, de facto, Secretary of State, following the death of Cardinal Maglione - recorded his reflections: "The acts of injustice and violence committed under his presidency weigh upon his priestly soul, dishonor his country, discredit the clergy and damage the Church also abroad...." The resulting telegram, drafted under Tardini's direction, bears corrections in the hand of Pius XII, indicating of course that it was seen by the Pontiff before it was dispatched. The October 29 telegram informed Burzio that his message had caused great pain to the Holy Father. It directed him to proceed immediately to President Tiso to inform him of the Pope's anguish: "Go at once to President Tiso and, informing him of His Holiness's deep sorrow on account of sufferings which very large numbers of persons — contrary to principles of humanity and justice — are undergoing in that nation on account of their nationality or race, in the name of the august Pontiff bring him back to sentiments and resolutions in conformity with his priestly dignity and conscience."

The Vatican soon received, via the British minister, a communication from the Czech government in London expressing its confidence in the efficacy of a Vatican intervention for Czechs and Jews. The Vatican's November 2 reply included a review of the Holy See's past and present actions. After recalling its "energetic protests" to the Slovak government, particularly in 1941-42, the Vatican note to the British minister concluded: "The Holy See, moved by those sentiments of humanity and Christian charity that always inspire its work in favor of those who are suffering, without distinction of religion, nationality or race, will continue also in the future, in spite of the growing difficulties of communications, to follow with particular attention the fate of the Jews of Slovakia, and will do everything in its power to bring them relief."

Unique Mission

On November 4, Burzio went as ordered to President Tiso on a mission that surely few apostolic nuncios have ever performed in modern times. The priest-president said he would give his own answer in writing to the Pope. Five days later Dr. Tiso summoned the papal charge' and gave him a letter, handwritten in Latin, which clarified his attitude and the position of his government toward the Jewish question. It arrived in Rome on December 19.

Among the Jews facing deportation in October was a group of about 400 persons in possession of passports from the United States and various Latin American countries. On October 7, following an appeal from the United States, the Secretariat of State had sent a note on their behalf to Karol Sidor, the Slovak minister. On November 21, an additional telegram was sent to the charge' in Bratislava, with the instruction: "The Holy See relies greatly on your deep interest and that of the episcopate in order that, in conformity with the universal mission of charity of the Church, all possible influence may be exerted on that government so that any Jews who are still in Slovak territory may be treated in a humane and Christian way."

What happened in fact was that the 400 had been taken under the special protection of the Slovak foreign ministry and brought to a separate shelter a Marianka, under the vigilance not of the German SS but of the Slovak gendarmerie. Nevertheless, they were again seized by the Germans and their passports declared forgeries. Only four were recognized as having authentic U.S. papers and returned to Marianka, where they were joined by the pitiful remnants of another raid, making a total of 13. They too were soon removed to Germany.

On November 21, having learned of the deportations, the Holy See notified Sidor of its indignation at the failure of the Slovak government to maintain its pledge. The Vatican note concluded:

> This news, in contradiction with the assurances referred to above, has been learned with deep sorrow by the Holy See which, once more, finds itself in the painful necessity of expressing its regret. The Holy See hopes that the Slovak government, in accordance with the principles of the Catholic religion, to which the vast majority of the people belongs, will leave no stone un-

turned in order that the Jews who are still in the territory of the Republic may not be subjected to even more sufferings.

The Action of the Holy See
for the Jews of Europe:
France

Confined in the German concentration camp at Vittel, France, were more Jews who claimed citizenship of either the United States or Latin American nations. They, too, were the objects of protracted and intensive diplomatic negotiations, with the Holy See as a willing participant. According to a report filed December 31, 1943, by the Nuncio Bernardini, they had been transferred from Germany to France, where they were kept together in the ostensible hope that they could be exchanged for Germans interned in the Western hemisphere. However, because in many cases their documents appeared to have been illegally obtained, one Latin American government after another withdrew its recognition of the passports, causing the prisoner's fragile situation to grow increasingly grave.

On December 27, 1943, the apostolic delegate in Washington wired his superiors that the Union of Orthodox Rabbis of the United States and Canada had pleaded for lenience toward the thousands of Polish Jews interned at Vittel. The Vatican, under Maglione's signature, immediately appealed to the Spanish government, the protecting power, urging it to maintain its support. And instructions were sent to Paraguay, one of the most involved states, to urge that rejection of the documents be suspended. On January 24, following contacts with the International Red Cross, the Vatican sent circular instructions to the other nunciatures in

Latin America, instructing them to solicit from the respective governments continued recognition of the passports, "no matter how illegally obtained."

The controversy over the Latin America passports seemed to subside for a short time. But on March 20, 1944, a German order set the stage for the transfer of the affected prisoners to the infamous camp at Drancy. From Madrid, alerted by Rome, the Nuncio Gaetano Cicognani on April 12 telegraphed that the German government did not welcome Spanish intervention for Jews (other than for Sephardic Jews, whose Spanish citizenship the Madrid government recognized). "However," stated the nuncio, "with regard to the Jews at Vittel this government will take opportune steps in view of an exchange between German civilians interned in America and Jews."

America Steps In

A few days later, the United States government finally moved to intervene. On April 18, the apostolic delegate in Washington reported that "government personalities and representative of Jewish organizations" had assured him that the U.S. government was ready to assist those Jews at Vittel, once released; that is, if they were allowed to leave France, presumably to Spain. But on April 26, Nunvio Bernardini said the Spanish intervention was insufficient and inefficacious. Worse yet, those Jews had been transferred to Drancy.

The desperate race against the clock continued. On May 16, the War Refugee Board came to the Delegate Cicognani with a new and belated proposal. They urged that the Jews, estimated to total 238, be returned to Vittel from Drancy on Spanish initiative. Maglione, despite his grounds for serious misgivings, issued the instructions. On May 20, he informed the Madrid nuncio of the appeal, adding: "I am aware of the difficulty of obtaining what is requested; however, I beg Your Excellency to consider if it is possible to take any further step in this direction."

With the landing of the Allies in France on June 6, no further correspondence on this subject was possible.

The Action of the Holy See
for the Jews of Europe:
Hungary

In 1944, the epicenter of the Jewish tragedy passed to Hungary. In this country, despite the enactment of severe anti-Semitic laws earlier, the Jews enjoyed relative safety beyond Nazi control. The Hungarian government of the Regent, Admiral Nicholas Horthy, did not hand over to the Germans any of its Jews, not even the many refugees from Poland and Slovakia. Hence, the consternation of the world Jewish community when on March 23, 1944, German troops marched into Hungary on the pretext of safeguarding communications. Budapest and it environs remained under the Regent's control until October, but wholesale deportations to Auschwitz from outlying parts of the country began in mid-May. The deportations were interrupted in early June when Admiral Horthy temporarily regained control. However, the Germans arrested Horthy in October, putting control of all Hungary in the hands of the fanatical anti-Semites of the Arrow Cross movement, and the massacre of the Jews was resumed. A third stage in the German reign of horror was the deportation of the remaining Jews not to Auschwitz but for labor in Austria — a useless and heartless death march. Not until December 23, 1944, did the Eichmann Kommando leave Budapest.

The Holy See's participation in the efforts to save the Hungarian Jews relative to the tragic months of 1944 is massively documented in the pages of Volume 10, here reviewed, of the *Acts and Documents of the Holy See Relative to the Second World War*. The general outline of the Holy See's actions on behalf of the Jews of Hungary is already known from other sources, but the newly edited documentation chronicles with precision the day-by-day, week-by-week interventions of the Holy See and its nuncio, His Excellency Angelo Rotta, in behalf of the imperiled Jews. Those actions are notable for their coordination with the hopes and plans of the many Jewish organizations which followed with passion the unfolding of the tragedy.

As 1944 began, concern for Hungary was largely limited to the Polish Jews who had taken refuge in the country. On January 29, the Apostolic Delegate Cicognani in Washington transmitted an appeal from the World Jewish Congress, asking the Holy See to use its influence with the Hungarians to permit the Polish refugees to be aided with money sent from the United States. But the March 23 German takeover drastically altered that situation. On March 25, the Delegate Cicognani informed the Vatican that the War Refugee Board — a newly created governmental organization linking all the Jewish organizations in a common program of aid to Jews — urged the Holy See to take urgent measures to aid the nearly two million Jews of Hungary (and Romania) living under terror and persecution and now threat-ened with extinction. The Board, said Cicognani, urged the full cooperation of the nuncio in Budapest, Msgr. Rotta,and the Hungarian bishops. The War Refugee Board's message was immed-iately transmitted to Buda-pest. In his March 28 reply, the Cardinal Secretary of State reminded the Washington Delegate that the Holy See had been constantly alert to the problem. The nuncios in Budapest and Bucharest, he said, would be instructed to take yet further appropriate action on behalf of the Jews in those countries. He warned, however, that the chances of significant accomplishment were slim.

More Jewish Appeals

The spontaneous turning to Rome was not limited to Jewish organizations in the United States. On March 31, a message arrived in the Vatican from the Chief Rabbi of Palestine, Rabbi Herzog, who addressed himself to the Holy See through Msgr. Roncalli, the apostolic delegate in Istanbul. On March 30, the nuncio transmitted an appeal from the Swiss Jewish Committee. and on that same day, the Delegate Godfrey transmitted an appeal from the Chief Rabbi of London, Dr. Hertz. On April 1, the British minister, Sir d'Arcy Osborne, submitted his government's request that the Holy See use its influence to prevent Jewish "refugees" in Hungary from being turned over to the Germans. Actually, it was not just the refugees who were in danger but the entire indigenous Jewish population.

From Budapest itself, the first information returned by Archbishop Rotta was fairly reassuring. For the moment, he telegraphed on March 31, there seemed to be no immediate danger of a persecution of the Jews. But he foresaw a bitter struggle and reported that many Jews had already been arrested. In the first days after the takeover, the nuncio was particularly concerned about the effect of the new anti-Semitic regulations on the status of the many baptized Jews in Hungary. But in keeping with his instructions from the Holy See, his position was amply clear; for the baptized Jews he insisted (not very successfully) that they have all the rights of non-Jewish Catholics, and for the others of Jewish origin, he demanded that they be treated according to the norms of fundamental human rights. In the coming months, with the emergence of a truly disastrous situation and under the impact of numerous queries and instructions from Rome, the nuncio was to engage increasingly in activities on behalf of the second category of victims of Hungarian anti-Semitism.

The first deportations to Auschwitz began on May 14. On the following day, the nuncio wrote two letters of protest, one to Dome Sztojay, the prime minister who was also foreign minister, the other to the Foreign Ministry itself. "The very fact of persecuting men merely on account of their racial origin," Rotta wrote to Sztojay, "is a violation of the natural law. If God has given them life, no one in the world has the right to take it from them or refuse them the means of preserving it, unless they have committed crimes. But to take anti-Semite measures, not taking into account at all the fact that many Jews have become Christians through reception of baptism, is a serious offense against the Church and in contradiction with the character of the Christian state, such as Hungary is proud to profess itself, even today."

In the note to the Foreign Ministry, Rotta complained: "Up to now all steps (for the baptized Jews) have been to no avail; on the contrary — as far as the nunciature knows — it is planned to arrive at the deportation (even if the reality is disguised) of hundreds of thousands of persons. Everyone knows what a deportation means in practice."

At this stage, of course, neither the nuncio nor the Jewish community in Budapest knew the real destination or fate of the deportees. But word of the new measure quickly spread beyond the country, and on May 17 the Vatican heard from the apostolic delegate in Washington that, according to a War Refugee Board report, deportations had begun to "an unknown destination." Cicognani reported that the Board was counting on intervention by the Holy See. To the ensuing Vatican query, Msgr. Rotta reported on May 24 that he had protested strongly in defense of the Jews, especially for those baptized, and against the ca-mouflaged deportation. In the meantime, he stated, the deportations were continuing as "forced labor" and carried out with systematic police brutality.

Msgr. Rotta Rebuffed

As expected, the Foreign Ministry's reply to Rotta's may 15 note was sharply negative. It scoffed at the religious sincerity of the converts from Judaism, and besides, it said, the problem was one of race, which is not changed by baptism. The question of the deportations was avoided by a patent falsehood - the Jews were being sent for labor. "It is not at all a question of deportation," the Foreign Minister said, "and all the necessary measures will be taken in order that their transportation will be carried out if possible in the company of their families, under humane conditions."

Fortified with strong backing from the Cardinal Secretary of State, received on May 29, the nuncio wrote a letter, dated June 5, which was strong by any diplomatic standards:

> In the meantime and to its deepest regret, the Apostolic Nunciature has been informed, and by a reliable source, about the conclusions of a recent conference, at which it was decided to deport all Hungarian Jews, without distinction of religion....According to other information, also absolutely reliable, deportation is already being carried out and with such methods that a number of persons succumb even before reaching the place of deportation.....

On the theme of deportation, Rotta continued:

> It is said that it is not a question of deportation, but of compulsory labor. It is possible to discuss about the words; but the reality is the same. When old men of over 70 and even over 80, old women, children and sick persons are taken away, one wonders for what work these human beings can be used? The reply given is that Jews

have been given the possibility of taking their families with them; but then the departure of the latter should be a matter of free choice. And what is to be said of cases in which these old people, sick people, etc., are the only ones deported, or when there is no relative whom they should follow? And when we think that Hungarian workers, who go to Germany for reasons of work, are forbidden to take their families, we are really surprised to see that this great favor is granted only to Jews.

Archbishop Rotta vigorously pressed his right and duty to protest particularly for those Jews who had become Catholics by baptism, and he rejected the allegation that their conversions were of dubious good faith. Reiterating his original position, he de-manded "that Christian Jews should be exempted from the anti-Semite provisions ... that all Jews should be treated in a humane way; and that even in the measures it will be necessary to take for the defense of the legitimate interests of the state, justice should always be safeguarded, as well as the fundamental rights of the human person."

Also transpiring during May and June were the negotiations between the Nazi chief of the deportations, Adolph Eichmann, and the head of the Jewish Rescue Committee in Hungary, Reszoe Kastner. On May 19, Joel Brand arrived in Istanbul bearing Eichmann's proposal to exchange the surviving Jews for 10,000 trucks.

Rotta's records give no indication that he or the Jewish community in Budapest knew the real significance of the wholesale expulsion of the Hungarian Jews. The brutality and secrecy accompanying the departees were enough to stigmatize the deportations as atrocities in themselves..

Meanwhile, the world Jewish community was active in its appeals. On June 1, the U.S. charge', Harold H. Tittmann, Jr., on instructions from his government, asked what the Holy See had done for the Jews of Hungary. On June 9, Cicognani reported from Washington that four important rabbis of the Emergency Committee to Save the Jewish People of Europe had addressed an anxious appeal to the Holy Father. It is known for certain, they said, that the extermination of Jews in Hungary had begun and was continuing. They asked the Pope to make a public appeal in the strongest possible terms to save these victims. The Hungarian Catholics, they said, would be impressed by an appeal from such a lofty source. On the same day, Rabbi Herzog of Palestine sent a similar message by way of the Delegate in Cairo, Arthur Hughes.

In reply to the resulting queries from Rome, Rotta could only confirm that 300,000 Jews had already been deported. it is rumored, he said in a June 18 telegram, that one-third of those had really been put to work outside of Hungary, but the fate of the remainder was still a matter of diverse speculation. Some responsible persons, he said, even speak of "annihilation camps." In any case, he said, the treatment of the deportees at departure was "truly ghastly." Direct intervention by the Holy See would be "extremely useful not to mention necessary," he said, especially since transports for new deportations were already standing ready.

On June 24, Rotta again wired the Vatican saying deportations were continuing and protests were unavailing. The faithful, said the nuncio, were surprised at the "inactivity" of the bishops. He again urged an appeal to the primate, Cardinal Seredi.

Also on June 24, the American charge' brought the Cardinal Secretary a message from the War Refugee Board. After recognizing that His Holiness had been sorely grieved by the "wave of hate" engulfing Europe and had labored unceasingly to inculcate a decent regard for the dignity of man, activated by a great compassion for the sufferings of a large portion of mankind, the message turned to Hungary.

The Pope's Telegram

Referring to the plan to deport 800,000 Jews in Hungary, the Board expressed its hope "...that His Holiness may find it appropriate to express himself on this subject to the authorities and people of Hungary, great numbers of whom profess spiritual adherence to the Holy See, personally by radio, through the nuncio and clergy in Hungary, as well as through a representative of the Holy See who might be specially dispatched to Hungary."

Editor's Note: (In his book, *While Six Million Died*, Arthur D. Morse puts forth a quite spurious version of this note from the War Refugee Board, and also gives it a false date, putting it some weeks earlier. "The Pope would wait a full month before sending his personal plea to Admiral Horthy," Morse writes. Actually, the Pope's note to Horthy is dated the day after receipt of the American appeal).

The flurry of Vatican correspondence in May and June culminated in the famous open telegram of June 25 sent by Pius XII to the Regent of Hungary, Admiral Horthy. It has long been supposed that the papal message was sent because of the "Auschwitz Protocol," which was transmitted in May by the charge' in Bratislava, the Nuncio Burzio. The relevant Vatican papers now demonstrate, however, that the memorandum containing the most authoritative and detailed description of the gas chambers at Auschwitz did not in fact reach the Vatican until late October, because Vatican couriers had been cut off since the Allied occupation of Rome.

The papal telegram to Horthy, according to the papers of the Secretariat of State of His Holiness, had already been drafted on June 12. Its preparation was the product of the incessant warnings and appeals from Rotta and the Jewish organizations. Most influential of all, perhaps, was Rotta's May 24 telegram suggesting a "passo diretto" by the Holy See.

Putting aside the War Refugee Board's suggestions that he make a personal radio appeal or send an envoy to Budapest, Pope Pius XII enacted his own plan, which proved successful. His June 25 "open" telegram to Admiral Horthy read as follows:

> We are being beseeched in various quarters to do everything in our power in order that, in this noble and chivalrous nation, the sufferings, already so heavy, endured by a large number of unfortunate people, because of their nationality or race, may not be extended and aggravated. As our Father's heart cannot remain insensitive to these pressing supplications by virtue of our ministry of charity which embraces all men, we address Your Highness personally, appealing to your noble sentiments in full confidence that you will do everything in your power that so many unfortunate people may be spared other afflictions and other sorrows.

The combination of factors that caused Admiral Horthy to reassert his authority and order the suspension of the deportation is, of course, beyond the scope of this review of Volume 10 of the *Actes.* Among those factors, though, were a press campaign launched in Switzerland, followed by an outpouring of messages from world leaders and the July 5 announcement by British Foreign Minister Sir Anthony Eden that the British radio would be employed to warn the Hungarian leaders. The Pope's open telegram, however, was the first of such protests to be sent to Horthy.

The suspension of the deportations had many causes - including the bombing of Budapest — but the vigilance of the papal nuncio, Angelo Rotta, his repeated protests and finally, the papal tele-gram can be said to have been of no small importance in this denouement. The Jewish organizations and the War Refugee Board, as their messages published in the *Actes* demonstrate, readily acknowledged the salutary effect of the papal intervention.

The Action of the Holy See
for the Jews of Europe:
Hungary after Horthy

The nightmare was, alas, far from over. Not only were sur-reptitious deportations carried out by the Eichmann Kommando, but atrocities on Hungarian soil redoubled. Horthy's days were numbered, and his power diminished pro-gressively under German pressure. Rumors of a forthcoming renewal of deportations grew. This time the nuncio adopted a new approach: As dean of the diplomatic corps in Budapest, he mobilized the heads of the four other neutral diplomatic missions for a joint protest. On August 21, Rotta and the envoys from Sweden, Spain, Portugal and Switzerland presented their remonstrances, declaring: "The undersigned representatives of the Neutral Powers accredited in Budapest have learned with a sentiment of painful surprise that the deportations of the Jews of Hungary are to begin again soon. They are also informed — and by absolutely reliable sources — what deportation means in most cases, even if it is disguised under the name of work abroad."

The five diplomats said the deportations were "unjust in their motive - for it is absolutely inadmissible that men should be persecuted and put to death just because of their racial origin -and brutal in their execution." This phraseology, already used by the nuncio, indicates that the joint message was drafted by Rotta too.

With military and political events of great portent rushing to their ultimate conclusion, conditions soon worsened for the Jews in Hungary. On October 15, Horthy, trying to reach an armistice with the Soviets, was arrested by the Germans. Hungary then came under the control of the fanatical anti-Semites of the Arrow Cross movement, with Ferenc Szalasi as Prime Minister. In the face of this new disaster, the Jewish organizations renewed their appeals to the Pope.

Papal Address

In an October 25 communication, the War Refugee Board reverted to the earlier proposal for a papal address by Vatican Radio in which the Holy Father would exhort the Hungarians to aid the Jews by hiding them and otherwise opposing the deportation. Again, however, Pius XII had a different way to the same end. His clue was provided by Rotta, who reported on October 22 that a collection for the "refugees" would be taken up in all the churches during the following week. On the day before the planned collections, an unusual papal message went by telegram to Cardinal Seredi. It seemed like an ordinary telegram of circumstance, but the Pope began by stating: "...urgent appeals continue to reach us from this nation imploring our intervention for the defense of persons exposed to persecution and violence because of their religious confession, or their race or their political convictions...." The Pope added his support to the call of the Hungarian bishops and concluded, "We form wishes that, in conformity with principles of humanity and justice, sufferings of this redoubtable conflict, already extremely serious, may not become even graver." The primate of Hungary may have been surprised to receive that unsolicited and unprecedented papal telegram, but he could not have missed the meaning of its opening reference to the racial question.

On November 10, the nuncio called on the new Hungarian foreign minister, Kemeny. According to the record of that meeting, discovered by the Allies after the war, Rotta wanted answers to four questions: Why had the Ministry of the Interior, again despite the promises of the prime minister, failed to recognize travel passes and protection letters? And why had there occurred the gravest of atrocities in the areas placed under the protection of the foreign diplomatic missions? Of course, no consistent answers were forthcoming.

The indefatigable nuncio appeared at the government offices again on November 17, this time with Swedish Ambassador Danielson for an audience with Prime Minister Szalasi. Summarizing the meeting and its results in a November 27 report, Rotta said, "No practical result was hoped for, in view of the mentality made up of religious ignorance and fanatical hatred of the Jews among the mass of the Arrow Cross." In that report, the nuncio informed the Vatican that he had issued 13,000 "Letters of Protection" which have "served some purpose at least to prevent for a certain time many Jews and especially baptized Jewish women from being deported." Rotta did not explain to his chiefs in Rome how the Vatican "protection letters" operated, except that they did help. In fact, those documents, like others issued at the same time by the other neutral diplomatic missions, became a sort of *habeas corpus* for many.

The terrible death march to Hegyeshalom on the Austrian border occurred in the final days of Nazi control of Hungary. On December 8, Rotta sent the Vatican what he described as a "promemoria presented to me on this matter by a religious sent by the nunciature as far as the frontiers of Hungary to relieve the sufferings of the wretched deportees and especially the ones protected by the nunciature."

Horrors Described

The unidentified narrator, witness and rescuer began his recital in this way: "Only Dostoevsky's pen would be capable of describing the horrors that accompany deportation from Budapest to Hegyeshalom, the frontier station. Going there by lorry, you pass group after group of deportees dragging themselves along, starving, frozen, limping, exhausted...."

By the end of December, Soviet forces encircled half of Budapest, but the anti-Jewish measures continued until the end. On December 24, 1944, the five neutral diplomatic missions joined in another, final protest. The government had decided to enclose all Jews in a ghetto, thereby of course, driving them from whatever shelter they had found in various embassies, religious houses and other hospital centers. In their general remonstrance, the diplomats urged that at least children and their mothers should be permitted to remain. This document was sent to Rome by the nuncio months later, with no account of the outcome.

Gotterdammerung?

During the last months of the war, as the Reich crumbled, there spread through Europe a sensational alarm concerning the Nazis' reported intention to exterminate all foreigners under their control. Though the report was taken seriously by the allied governments, it was never confirmed after the war, so it has passed into obscurity largely ignored by historians. But, as the documents show, the Holy See was caught up in this final burst of fear of a climactic Nazi atrocity.

The Vatican learned of the warning through Polish Ambassador Casimir Papee on September 25, 1944. All the inmates of Auschwitz were to be liquidated, he said. Accordingly, on the next day, the nuncio in Berlin was asked to intervene in whatever way he judged most effective. This time the Secretariat did not ask him to first verify the report. The Holy See told him it had been informed "that German authorities were preparing a massacre of prisoners in Auschwitz concentration camp. These prisoners, accused of 'political crimes,' are said to amount to 45,000, mainly Poles, but also Italians and other nationalities."

Several days later, the Apostolic Delegate in Washington reported that a group of Jewish spokesmen had asked for a papal appeal to the German government and to the German people "as the only means to save the existence" of the Jews and in particular, the 45,000 Jews and Christians of Polish, French and Czech nationality, interned at Auschwitz and in imminent danger of death. Later, Cicognani amended his telegram, adding the camp of Birchenau-Nauss [sic]. The Red Cross of Geneva had reportedly appealed to the Germans too. In an October 18 telegram from Washington, Cicognani said, "situation deportees in Germany already distressing, if events precipitate it might become tragic and end in a bloodbath."

On October 13, Orsenigo reported from Berlin that the reports, according to the Wilhelmstrasse, were Allied propaganda. Orsenigo himself commented in his report: "though admitting sincerity of the (of the) Foreign Ministry, it is not excluded that the notorious SS formations have received secret instructions that are very different."

After subsiding somewhat, the alarm revived again in the last months of the war. On January 25, 1945, Tardini warned Orsenigo again, after receiving information from the Polish ambassador. On March 3, 1945, Orsenigo was instructed to take steps to assure the safety of prisoners, deportees, internees and foreign laborers, but at that late date, from his remote base at Eichstatt, there was little that Orsenigo could do. On March 18, the delegate in Washington reported that the Jews in America were "terrified" at the report that all Jews in German hands, estimated at 600,000, would be liquidated. In his March 28 reply, Tardini recounted the Vatican's efforts to forestall such a tragedy. Responding to rumors that Germans would be sent to labor in Russia, he said such a move would not be the very best way to prevent further massacres of Jews and Poles.

Concluding Observations

Failures and lack of success do not in any way detract from the merit of the good effort. Of rejections and disappointments, the Holy See experienced many, as indeed did also the many and varied Jewish organizations and men of devotion who saw their struggles reduced to saving the small minority of victims lucky enough to be in a special position, while witnessing, helplessly, the daily massacre of the vast majority.

As Professor Burkhart Schneider said in his concluding remarks to Volume 9 of the *Actes,* "For the right understanding also of this volume of documents, it must be considered that it is impossible to reconstruct the whole picture of events from the *Actes* alone, even when they exist and are published in such a large number. What is preserved in writing and transmitted is often only a pale shadow of the reality. And if that is true in general, it applies all the more in the field of charitable activities, which the Church tried to develop. For charity and its initiatives pass unnoticed, to a fair extent, when it is a question of a scientific collection of data, which is necessarily dry and detached."

To that should be added one further observation on the question of the meaning of papal action. It has been said — and even recently, in a book by an American priest (*Vatican Diplomacy and the Jews during the Holocaust, 1939-1943,* by John F. Morley, KTAV Publishing House, New York, 1980) — that the Holy See was concerned only with the safety of Catholic Jews and not with the safety of other Jews. This view is certainly unhistoric and is contradicted not only in this, Volume 10 of the *Actes,* but in those that pre-ceded. The close and constant collaboration of the leading world Jewish organizations with the Holy See in matters concerning the Jews, and the close relationships between the nuncios and the local leaders of the Jewish communities, are eloquent witness that the Holy See did in fact carry out its humanitarian mission "without distinction of nationality, religion or race." To say otherwise is to do violence to the historical record and to perpetrate a gratuitous denigration of a great humanitarian and Pope.

Epilogue

When an armed force ruled well-nigh omnipotent, and morality was at its lowest ebb, Pius XII commanded none of the former and could only appeal to the latter, in confronting, with bare hands, the full might of evil.

A sounding protest, which might turn out to be self-thwarting - or quiet piecemeal rescue? Loud words — or prudent deeds? The dilemma must have been sheer agony, for whatever course he chose, horrible consequences were inevitable. Unable to cure the sickness of an entire civilization, and unwilling to bear the brunt of Hitler's fury, the Pope, unlike many far mightier than he, alleviated, relieved, retrieved, appealed, petitioned — and saved as best he could by his own lights.

Who, but a prophet or a martyr could have done much more?...

The Talmud teaches us that "whosoever preserves one life, it is accounted to him by Scripture as if he had preserved a whole world."

If this is true — and it is as true as that most Jewish of tenets, the sanctity of human life — then Pius XII deserves that forest in the

Judean hills which kindly people in Israel proposed for him in October, 1958. A memorial forest, like those planted for Winston Churchill, King Peter of Yugoslavia and Count Bernadotte of Sweden — with 860,000 trees.

Pinchas Lapide
Three Popes and the Jews
New York, Hawthorne, 1967,
pages 267-269)

A QUESTION
OF JUDGMENT:
PIUS XII
AND
THE JEWS

Dr. Joseph L. Lichten, who died in Rome, in December, 1987, was a long-time proponent of mutual understanding and cooperation between the Catholic and Jewish communities in both the United States and Europe. He was born in Poland, received his Doctor of Law degree from the University of Warsaw, and engaged in international diplomacy with the Polish government. In 1963, shortly after the initial production of Rolf Hochhuth's play, *The Deputy,* and while serving as director of the International Affairs Department for the Anti-Defamation League of B'nai B'rith, he wrote this monograph. It was published by the National Catholic Welfare Conference, forerunner of the United States Catholic Conference. It is reproduced here in its entirety.

A Question of Judgment: Pius XII and the Jews

by Joseph L. Lichten

In any human organization, the actions and attitudes of its leader color the image the organization has of itself and projects to those outside its membership. The stronger the leader, in his vested authority and in his person, the more firmly will this image be molded in his form.

This truism is particularly applicable to the Roman Catholic Church. Men speak of "good" popes and "bad," and of "good" and "bad" ages in the history of the Church. The judgments used to define these nebulous value words vary according to the judge's own culture, standards, faith or lack of it, and other equally subtle abstractions; Terence said it succinctly in *Phormio* (II, 4, 14): *"Quot homines, tot sententiae."*

Recently an indictment has been brought down on Pope Pius XII, and by extension on the Catholic Church, of criminal implication in the extermination of some six million Jews during World War II. The principal accuser, in terms of publicity at least, does not present very convincing credentials, though he states his case persuasively. More important, it is Vatican practice not to open its archives on any period in history until several decades have passed. Therefore, the richest single source of information on Pope Pius XII's actions during his reign cannot be tapped.

Nonetheless, the question that has been raised has enormous significance; and it demands examination. One personal comment: many times, while searching through the appropriate documentation, I was also searching my soul. In view of my personal tragedy, I have a special obligation to scrutinize every detail related to the Jewish tragedy of the last war.

What is the case against Pius XII? In brief, that as head of one of the most powerful moral forces on earth he committed an unspeakable sin of omission by not issuing a formal statement condemning the Nazis' genocidal slaughter of the Jews, and that his silence was motivated by reasons considered in modern times as base: political exigency, economic interests, and personal ambition.

What is the case for him? That in relation to the insane behavior of the Nazis, from overlords to self-styled cogs like Eichmann, he did everything humanly possible to save lives and alleviate suffering among the Jews; that a formal statement would have provoked the Nazis to brutal retaliation, and would substantially have thwarted further Catholic action on behalf of Jews. To the Sacred College of Cardinals Pius XII wrote on June 2, 1943: "Every word that We addressed to the responsible authorities and every one of Our public declarations had to be seriously weighed and considered in the interest of the persecuted themselves in order not to make their situation unwittingly even more difficut and unbearable."[1]

The defense and the prosecution, to extend the metaphor, have both stated their positions strongly and publicly, taking the material for their arguments from as much of the record of Pius XII's activities as is now known, from knowledge of the Pope's character, and from personal recollections.

There is considerable documentation in support of Pope Pius' fear that a formal statement would worsen, not improve, conditions for the persecuted. Ernst von Weizsacker, the German ambassador to the Vatican during World War II, wrote in his memoirs:

> Not even institutions of worldwide importance, such as the International Red Cross or the Roman Catholic Church saw fit to appeal to Hitler in a general way on behalf of the Jews or to call openly on the sympathies of the world. It was precisely because they wanted to help the Jews that these organizations refrained from making any general and public appeals; for they were afraid that they would injure rather than help the Jews thereby. [2]

Pius XII's "silence," let us remember, extended to persecutions of Catholics as well. Despite his intervention, 3000 Catholic priests were murdered by the Nazis in Germany, Austria, Poland, France, and other countries; Catholic schools were shut down, Catholic publications were forced out of print or strictly censored, and Catholic churches closed. The possibility of a public statement from the Vatican moved German Foreign Secretary Joachim von Ribbentrop to wire von Weizsacker on January 24, 1943:

Should the Vatican either politically or propagandistically oppose Germany, it should be made unmistakably clear that worsening of relations between Germany and the Vatican would not at all have an adverse effect on Germany alone. On the contrary, the German government would have sufficient effective propaganda material as well as retaliatory measures at its disposal to counteract each attempted move by the Vatican. [3]

Pius learned precisely how firm this German threat was from the protest of the Dutch bishops against seizures of the Jews, for immediately following that protest and, as later confirmed by an SS officer, in direct answer to it, the Nazis stepped up their anti-Jewish activities in the Netherlands; a week after the pastoral letter was read at all the masses in Holland, the SS rounded up every priest and monk and nun who had any "Jewish blood" whatever, and deported them to concentration camps.[4] Pius and his bishops and nuncios in Nazi-occupied or -dominated countries knew that, like a sane man faced with a gun-carrier threatening to shoot, Hitler and his cohorts could not be considered civilized human beings. As Archbishop Andrea Cassulo, papal nuncio in Romania, said in June, 1942, "I must proceed cautiously because [my actions] could ruin, instead of being useful to, so many wretched persons whom I must often listen to and help." [5]

The Pope's decision to refrain from a formal condemnation of the Nazi's treatment of Jews was approved by many Jews. One Berlin couple, Mr. and Mrs. Wolfsson, came to Rome after having been in prison and concentration camps. They took shelter in a convent of German nuns while Pius himself, whom they had seen during an audience, arranged for them to escape to Spain. Recalling those terrible days, the Wolfssons recently declared:

None of us wanted the Pope to take an open stand. We were all fugitives, and fugitives do not wish to be pointed at. The Gestapo would have become more excited and would have intensified its inquisitions. If the Pope had protested, Rome would have become the center of attention. It was better that the Pope said nothing. We all shared this opinion at the time, and this is still our conviction today.[6]

In a letter in the London *Times* of May 15, 1963, Sir Alec Randall, a former British representative at the Vatican, comments:

Others besides Pius XII had to face a similar agonizing dilemma. The Polish cardinal, Prince Sapieha, begged Pius XII not to make public protests, as they only increased the persecution of his people. The International Red Cross refrained from protest because they feared that their work in German-controlled countries would be stopped. The British and American Governments were accused of callous indifference to the fate of the Jews because they failed to take them out of Nazi clutches before it was too late. To have done what was asked of them would have prolonged the war.

Pius XII's defenders in print — among others Sir D'Arcy Osborne, Msgr. Alberto Giovanetti, Father Robert Leiber, and Harry Greenstein,[7] who represent three faiths and four nationalities — point to two elements of the Pope's personal philosophy in addition to the pragmatic reason for his decision to refrain from an explicit condemnation of the Nazis. First he considered it his paramount duty to be pastor of the Universal Church, and in his eyes this position required the strictest impartiality. Second, as an experienced diplomat, he knew full well that the days when a Vatican sanction carried weight were long since past, as Sir Alec Randall points out:[8] we have already seen just how correct this appraisal was. The era of renewed spiritual and moral leadership introduced by the pontificate of John XXIII had not yet dawned.

The undercurrent of all the Pope did was embodied in his words to Archbishop Angelo Roncalli, later to become Pope John, when the papal nuncio came from Istanbul to visit Pius XII: "above all else comes the saving of human lives."[9]

One of the strongest testimonials to Pius' great feeling for Jews comes from an unpublished interview I had with Dr. Herman Datyner, a distinguished urologist. In 1940 Dr. Datyner, helped by his numerous international contacts, escaped from Warsaw into Italy, where, like all Jews and foreigners, he was arrested. He was sent from one camp to another and spent a total of four years interned. Orders were sent to these camps, but each instruction was sabotaged or thwarted, and it was known among the internees that the intervention on their behalf had come directly from the Vatican.

In 1945, as a member of the Inter-Allied Conference for Refugees and a special representative of all Jewish refugee groups and organizations in Italy, Dr. Datyner asked for and received an audience with Pius XII in order to thank the Supreme Pontiff for his help and care during the war years. He memorized a part of Pius' conversation, and repeats it with emotion today:

> Yes, I know, my son, all the sufferings of you Jews. I am sorry, truly sorry, about the loss of your family. I suffered a great deal, . . . knowing about Jewish sufferings, and I tried to do whatever was in my power in order to make your fate easier. . . . I will pray to God that happiness will return to you, to your people. Tell them this.

The prosecution has rallied behind a young German playwright named Rolf Hochhuth, whose play, *Der Stellvertreter* (*The Representative*[*]), first performed in Berlin on February 20, 1963, and in London September 25, carries a message summed up in the words of its main protagonist, the young Jesuit Riccardo Fontana: "A Vicar of Christ who sees these things before his eyes and still remains silent because of state policies, who delays even one day . . . such a pope . . . is a criminal?"

To substantiate his accusation, Mr. Hochhuth adds 46 pages of documentation to the printed play,[10] and excerpts quotations from the writings of two well-known contemporary thinkers, among others: the Catholic Francois Mauriac and the Jew Leon Poliakov.

The documentation which the playwright presents has impressed a good many people, especially reviewers, most of whom mention this "factual substantiation" in their treatment of the play. Hochhuth's efforts are indeed commendable, though a student of the history of the period will notice — obviously — the bias created by lacunae (the playwright is only interested, of course, in supporting his thesis) and — more subtly — unjustified conclusions. An example is found on page 312 of the English edition of the play, where Hochhuth writes:

---

[*] Editor's Note: At the time Dr. Lichten wrote this book, the Rolf Hochhuth play "*Der Stellvertreter*" had been produced on the London stage as "The Representative." The title of the play as later produced in the United States would be "*The Deputy.*" The term "Stellvertreter" admits of several possible English renditions. Yet another variant appears on page 11 of the May, 1988 issue of "*30 Days,*" the American edition of the Italian Catholic monthly magazine "*30 Giorni.*" The play is there called "*The Vicar.*"

But what Donati reported to the Centre de Documentation Juive Contemporaine (Documents CC XVII-78) about the official attitude of the diplomats of the Holy See, should be quoted. In the autumn of 1942, Donati had a note referring to the situation of the Jews in Southern France delivered to the Pope through the agency of the Father General of the Capuchins, in which he asked for Papal assistance. It was not forthcoming.

The Centre de Documentation Juive Contemporaine in Paris contains abundant and thoroughly validated material on the relations between Angelo Donati, an Italian Jew to whom (as Hochhuth points out) many of his coreligionists owe their lives, and the Capuchin Father Marie-Benoit, as well as on the Vatican's actual response to pleas from Donati and others; I will summarize that material later in this article. Hochhuth's conclusion, "[Papal assistance] was not forthcoming," cannot be other than a deliberate distortion.

One of the several quotations which appear in the front of both the German and the English published versions of *The Representative* suffers from similar distortion. To Hochhuth's credit, when he was called to account on this matter, he promised to correct the English edition, which he has done. In the German printing, M. Mauriac is quoted as follows: "We have not yet had the consolation of hearing the successor to the Galilean Simon Peter condemn, unequivocally and clearly and not with diplomatic allusions, the crucifixion of these countless 'brothers of the Lord.' ... a crime of such magnitude falls in no small measure to the responsibility of those witnesses who never cried out against it — whatever the reason for their silence." However, the missing middle sentence — which Hochhuth reinstates in the English edition of the play — reads: "No doubt the occupying forces were able to bring irresistible pressure to bear, no doubt the silence of the Pope and his cardinals was a most terrible duty; the important thing was to avoid even worse misfortunes."[11] Mauriac, like Poliakov, as we shall see, was obviously not blind to the incredible dilemma Pope Pius found himself in, Hochhuth's selective quotation not-withstanding.

Dr. Poliakov's emphasis, in his book *The Jews under the Italian Occupation* and elsewhere, has been the same; granted, Pius XII did extend help and comfort to the Jews — the record is quite clear on this score — but he did not do enough. This "enough" would have been a firm protest, a formal statement, from the Vatican against the German "solution of the Jewish problem." Yet Poliakov says also that "during the Hitler terror, the clergy acted untiringly and unceasingly to give humane help, with the approval and on the prompting of the Vatican." Furthermore:

> This direct aid given the persecuted Jews by the Pope in his capacity as bishop of Rome was the symbolic expression of an activity that was extended throughout the whole of Europe, encouraging and promoting the efforts put forth by the Catholic churches in the majority of countries. It is certain that secret instructions were sent out by the Vatican, urging the national churches to intervene in behalf of the Jews.[12]

These instructions, Poliakov adds, rendered special papal instructions or statements unnecessary. It is known that in 1940 Pius XII sent out a secret instruction to the Catholic bishops of Europe entitled *Opere et caritate* (*By Work and Love*). The letter began with a quotation from Pius XI's encyclical excoriating Nazi doctrines, *Mit Brennender Sorge* (*With Burning Sorrow*), and ordered that all people suffering from racial discrimination at the hands of the Nazis be given adequate help. The letter was to be read in churches with the comment that racism was incompatible with the teachings of the Catholic faith.

Poliakov's position, then, is essentially negative, though with noteworthy qualifications:

> The humanitarian activities of the Vatican were necessarily circumscribed with prudence and caution. The immense responsibilities on the Pope's shoulders and the powerful weapons the Nazis could use against the Holy See undoubtedly combined to prevent him from making a formal public protest, though the persecuted keenly hoped to hear one. It is sad to have to say that during the entire war, while the laboratories of death worked to capacity, the Pope kept his silence.[13]

It is a matter of record, of course, that Pope Pius XII did not launch a verbal attack directly against the Third Reich; the statements he did make during World War II, with rare exceptions, were general expressions of sorrow and sympathy for all victims of oppression of any kind, and did not name names. As Von Weizsacker wrote in a report to the Minister of Foreign Affairs in Berlin on October 28, 1943:

> Regardless of the advice of many, the Pope has not yet let himself be persuaded to make an official condemnation of the deportation of the Roman Jews. Despite the fact that he must expect his attitude to be criticized by our enemies and attacked by the Protestants in Anglo-Saxon countries, who will use it in their anti-Catholic propaganda, he has thus far achieved the impossible in these delicate circumstances in order not to put his relations with the German government and with its representatives at Rome to the test. Since it is currently thought that the Germans will take no further steps

against the Jews in Rome, the question of our relations with the Vatican may be considered closed.

In any case, it appears that such is the viewpoint of the Vatican. *L'Osservatore Romano* of October 25-26, however, published an official statement on the Pope's charitable activities. The statement, which was couched in the usual abstract and vague Vatican terminology, said that the Pope expressed his paternal solicitude for all men without regard to race, nationality, or religion. The many activities of the Pope would be increased because so many were suffering so much misfortune.

One could not raise any objection to this statement because few will recognize a direct reference to the Jewish problem in it.[14]

According to the March, 1961, article "Pius XII and the Jews, 1943-1944" in the Jesuit publication *Civilta Cattolica,* by Father Robert Leiber, Pius XII's personal assistant from 1924 to 1959, the Pope directly denounced an illegal procedure only once during the entire war; the German invasion of Holland, Belgium, and Luxemburg on May 10, 1940, prompted the now famous telegrams to the heads of the three invaded states. These messages aside, Pius XII followed the policy of Benedict XV during World War I, and protested in general terms against injustices and violence wherever these might be found.

But is it correct to say that Pius XII was otherwise silent on the subject of Nazi atrocities? Had he utterly ignored the plight of the Jews, the term would be appropriate; had he spoken directly in their cause, he might today be called foolhardy — if we are to carry even his accusers' admissions to their logical conclusion. In effect, he chose a third course, one dictated by his long experience as a Vatican statesman and his great desire to save lives.

Many persons have already taken up the dispute, and some of their comments will be quoted in the present article. Rolf Hochhuth was a child during the period in question; further, his primary motivation was to write a good play and not an accurate record, and his historic perspective — like that of us all — is insufficient for a just critique of Pius' actions. If he were the only accuser, we could dismiss the issue; too much noise has been made about Hochhuth's drama *qua* drama as it is. But the controversy, coming on the heels of Dr. Hannah Arendt's question of why the Jews did not defend themselves better, has drawn more thoughtful minds into its wake. Some Jewish leaders who had none but words of praise for Pius' efforts on behalf of the Jews now point fingers of blame at him, effectively reversing their position of fifteen and twenty years' standing.

I think it would be well to examine more closely the record, as far as we now know it, of what Pope Pius actually said and did, how his words and actions were received by both Catholics and non-Catholics, and — perhaps most important — what motives are attributed to him; for in our Western culture, motivation is an essential factor in any discussion of a man's probity.

That the Pope was deeply antagonistic to the racism the National-Socialists advocated is evident from his work prior to his election to the papacy. The famous *Mit Brennender Sorge* shows the hand of Pacelli, then Vatican Secretary of State; more directly, as papal legate, Pacelli spoke these scathing words to 250,000 pilgrims at Lourdes on April 28, 1935:

> They [The Nazis] are in reality only miserable plagiarists who dress up old errors with new tinsel. It does not make any difference whether they flock to the banners of the social revolution, whether they are guided by a false conception of the world and of life, or whether

they are possessed by the superstition of a race and blood cult.[15]

Pacelli had obviously established his position clearly, for the Fascist governments of both Italy and Germany spoke out vigorously against the possibility of his election to succeed Pius XI in March of 1939, though the cardinal secretary of state had served as papal nuncio in Germany from 1917 to 1929 and had been instrumental in the signing of a concordat between Germany and the Vatican. The day after his election, the Berlin *Morgenpost* said: "The election of Cardinal Pacelli is not accepted with favor in Germany because he was always opposed to Nazism and practically determined the policies of the Vatican under his predecessor."

As I wrote in the *Anti-Defamation League Bulletin* for October, 1958, the new Vicar of Christ showed no softening after his election toward Hitler's brutal policies; Pius the Pope was the same man as Pacelli the priest. Von Ribbentrop, granted a formal audience on March 11, 1940, went into a lengthy harangue on the invincibility of the Third Reich, the inevitability of a Nazi victory, and the futility of papal alignment with the enemies of the Fuhrer. Pius XII heard Von Ribbentrop out politely and impassively. Then he opened an enormous ledger on his desk and, in his perfect German, began to recite a catalogue of the persecutions inflicted by the Third Reich in Poland, listing the date, place, and precise details of each crime. The audience was terminated; the Pope's position was clearly unshakable.

Summi Pontificatus, the first encyclical of his pontificate, issued October 20, 1939, had strongly attacked the doctrines of totalitarianism, racism, and materialism. The encyclical read in part: "The first of these pernicious errors, today so widespread, is the disregard for that law of human solidarity and charity dictated and imposed . . . by the common origin and equality in their rational nature of all men, regardless of the people to which they belong."[16] In his Christmas Message of 1942 and in similar terms on June 2, 1943, he deplored the treatment of

> . . . hundreds of thousands of persons who, through no fault of their own and by the single fact of their nationality or race, have been condemned to death or to progressive extinction. . . . It is a consolation for Us that, through the moral and spiritual assistance of Our representatives and through Our financial assistance, We have been able to comfort a great many of the refugees, homeless, and emigrants, including non-Aryans.[17]

That assistance was of inestimable value. It can be divided roughly into the two categories Pius XII names in the above broadcast; the work of the Vatican's representatives — the nuncios, bishops, clergy and religious, and laymen — and the financial assistance and other material services rendered the persecuted either directly by the Vatican or through appeals from the Holy See.

On behalf of the Jews of Slovakia, Pius XII intervened directly and — contrary to the allegations of his accusers — in unambiguous terms. A government ordinance, called simply the Jewish Code, was passed on September 9, 1941, parroting the anti-semitic regulations of the Third Reich. A lengthy note was prepared by the Vatican Secretariat of State and transmitted on November 12 to the Slovak minister to the Holy See, Karl Sidor. It read in part:

... With the deepest sorrow the Holy See has learned that also in Slovakia, a country whose population almost totally honors the best Catholic tradition, a "Government Ordinance" was issued on September 9 establishing special "racial legislation" and containing various regulations in open contrast with Catholic principles.

In fact the Church, universal by the will of her divine Founder, welcomes to her bosom people of all races, and views all mankind with a maternal solicitude for the purpose of creating and developing among all men feelings of brotherhood and love, in accordance with the explicit and categoric teaching of the Gospel .... [18]

Five weeks earlier, the Slovak bishops had sent a protest note to Jozef Tiso, the President of the puppet state:

... It does not escape the attention of the careful examiner that the philosophical conception on the basis of which the present ordinance has been drawn up is the racist ideology.... We do not intend to enumerate here all the dangerous errors that this doctrine conceals in itself.... We wish only to recall that the materialistic theory of racism is in direct contradiction with the teaching of the Catholic Church on the common origin of all men from a single Creator and Father, on the substantial equality of men before God stressed especially by the Apostle of the peoples, on the Common supernatural destiny of men in consequence of the universal redemption work of Christ.... The so-called Jewish Code violates natural law and the freedom of individual conscience. [19]

This was but one of many protests directly from Pius XII or from the bishops against the persecution and deportation of Slovakian

Jews. These provoked Prime Minister Vojtech Tuka to write on Mar 3, 1943:

> It is incomprehensible to the government that ecclesiastic circles and especially the Catholic clergy should today adduce so many protests against the elimination of the Jews, who in the past were most responsible for the misery of the Slovak people . . . . The Slovak clergy — save for a few honorable exceptions — has rarely showed such zeal for the interests of its own people as it does now for the interests of the Jews, and in many cases even for those who are not baptized . . . .[20]

Despite this and other verbal rejections of the protests from the Catholic hierarchy, Pius' pleas were finally heeded; although 70,000 Jews had been deported from the new pro-Nazi republic, the papal nuncio in Bratislava succeeded in obtaining a promise from the puppet government that further deportation plans would largely be discarded. But when the Germans occupied Slovakia in early fall of 1944, the semblance of independence which that country had maintained for five years vanished, and with it the hard-won reprieves for the remaining Jewish population. Under the urging of the Vatican, the Slovak government protested the Nazis' familiar brutality toward the Jews, but to no avail. All the Pope could now do was continue to express his concern. A telegram sent in October to Archbishop Roncalli in Istanbul read that the Holy See, "despite the increasing difficulties, including those of communications, is still following with great attention the fate of the Jews in Slovakia and Hungary, and will leave nothing undone to help them."[21]

The papal nuncio in Romania, Monsignor Andrea Cassulo, exercised his considerable diplomatic and spiritual authority in behalf of the Jews throughout the war; he made his first formal efforts as early as February 16, 1941. He worked untiringly to win the government's permission to send Jewish orphans to Palestine, and with some success. On October 20 he registered an official protest with Mihail Antonescu, Minister of Foreign Affairs, against the government's admitted plans to "regulate the Jewish question," and came, through his repeated intercessions, to be known to the Jewish population of Romania as an ever-willing source of assistance.[22]

Because of his close contact with Romania's Chief Rabbi Safran throughout the war, Archbishop Cassulo kept himself and the Vatican informed about the condition of Romanian Jews, especially those interned in concentration camps beyond the Dnieper. In 1942 and 1943, prompted by Pope Pius XII, the nuncio visited numbers of camps, taking with him considerable sums of money sent by the Pope for distribution among the prisoners. Following the 1943 visit, the Archbishop presented a ten-point request to Rado Lecca, the government official in charge of Jewish affairs, to alleviate the misery in the camps; by June, 1943, Rabbi Safran was able to report to him that conditions had improved noticeably as a result.[23]

The Holy See's interest in the plight of the Romanian Jews is attested to by Archbishop Cassulo's own official messages and memoranda as well as the testimony of Rabbi Safran. On November 24, 1942, the apostolic nuncio sent Mihail Antonescu a note which read in part:

> Ever since the Romanian government has come to believe itself bound to examine the diverse aspects of the Jewish question in Romania and to solve it in accordance with the country's interests, the Holy See has been concerned, above all other considerations, with . .

. the respect that must be assured to every innocent person who is abandoned and without support . . . ."[24]

The note, written immediately after Archbishop Cassulo's return from a visit to Rome, came at a particularly dangerous time for Romania's Jews. The Third Reich was exerting heavy pressure for mass deportations of Jews eastward, to beyond the Bug River where German police were in command. In the opinion of many members of the diplomatic corps in Bucharest, the nuncio's applications were responsible for first the suspension of the deportation plans and then their postponement until the following year.[25] The Jewish community in Romania asked Archbishop Cassulo on February 14, 1943, to write their gratitude to Pius XII for the help of the Vatican and its nunciature.[26]

A Dr. Frederic, a young German Foreign Office agent, was sent on a tour through various Nazi-occupied and satellite countries to feel out their reaction to the Germans. As Frederic wrote in his confidential report to the German Foreign Office datelined Berlin, September 19, 1943, his meeting in Lwow with the Ukrainian leaders and Metropolitan Sheptytsky was far from heartening; the Metropolitan remained adamant in saying that the killing of Jews was "an inadmissible act," and Frederic comments, "In this issue the Metropolitan made the same statements and even used the same phrasing as the French, Belgian, and Dutch bishops, as if all of them were receiving the same instructions from the Vatican."[27]

The action taken to help the Jews in Hungary was manifold. In the spring of 1944, the papal nuncio, Msgr. Angelo Rotta, warned that country on the first day of the deportation of Jews that the whole world knew what they really signified; on June 25, 1944, he delivered Miklos Horthy a letter which was a strong protest from the Pope.[28] Prior to the onslaught on Hungarian Jews by the Fascists, Hungary responded to promptings from the Vatican and gave asylum to Jewish refugees from Poland and Slovakia. As the bloodbath swept Hungary, the Vatican notified its nuncios in Budapest and Bratislava to watch the situation and do all they could for the welfare of Jewish refugees.[29] At about the same time, the Pope had the following message sent to the World Jewish Congress, with which he was in communication during the war:

> Whenever reports reached the Holy See that the situation of the Jews in Hungary was becoming worse, steps were immediately taken to assist these people and to alleviate their condition. The Holy See gives assurance that it will continue to act in behalf of these Jews. Following instructions from the Holy See, the Apostolic Nunciature in Budapest has repeatedly intervened with the Hungarian authorities so that violent and unjust measures would not be taken against the Jews in that country. The bishops of Hungary have engaged in an intense activity in favor of persecuted Jews. The action on the part of the Nunciature and the bishops will continue as long as necessary... The Holy Father... [sent] a personal open telegram to the Cardinal [Archbishop of Strigonium (Esztergom)], and in this communication His Holiness again manifested his heartfelt interest in promoting the welfare of all those exposed to violence and persecution because of their race or religion or on account of political motives. The Holy Father gives assurance that he will, in the future as in the past, do everything in favor of these people in Hungary or in any other European country.[30]

The Pope's words, discreet as they are, give little indication of how intense the clergy's activity was. The nuncio spoke out sharply, as did the Hungarian bishops, and simultaneously undertook as widespread rescue measures as possible. Helped by priests and nuns, he and the bishops sheltered several thousand Jews, distributed false papers, and provided information, clothing, and food; Laszlo Endre, the Undersecretary of the Interior in the Nazi government, said testily that "as far as aid to the Jews is concerned, priests and clergy men . . . unfortunately are in the first rank. Protection and intervention have never been on such a large scale as today."[31]

The Catholic bishops of Holland published a pastoral letter read in all the Catholic churches throughout the country on April 19, 1942, condemning "the unmerciful and unjust treatment meted out to Jews by those in power in our country."[32] And in a telegram dated July 11, 1942, the bishops demanded the suspension of coercive measures against unchristened as well as christened Jews. But the deportations continued. On July 26, the bishops joined with representatives of almost all other religious communities to denounce the Nazis' lawless measures, but the response, as we have seen, was mass arrests of Catholics and Jews, among them Dr. Edith Stein, a convert to Catholicism and a nun, who was sent to Auschwitz.[33]

In France, as everywhere else that humans were being victimized by the Nazis, Pius XII's aim was to utilize the Vatican's spiritual and material resources as completely as possible to help the oppressed in their misery. His means were deliberately quiet; we know how strongly he felt that any direct attack by the Vatican on Axis policies would spell at least interference with and at worst complete contravention of the Church's activities. Yet his exhortations to Catholics to cleave to the humane principles of their religion, like his messages to his bishops to do all they could to help, within the limitations of local conditions, were quite clear in their implications. Late in June, 1943, the Vatican radio warned the French people, "He who makes a distinction between Jews and other men is unfaithful to God and is in conflict with God's commands."[34] Catholic bishops and priests had long since been following these promptings, as two 1942 pastoral letters attest. The first, from Archbishop (later Cardinal) Jules Gerard Saliege of Toulouse and read on August 23, strongly echoed the principles stressed over and over by Pius:

> There is a Christian morality ... that confers rights and imposes duties. These duties and these rights come from God. One can violate them. But no mortal has the power to suppress them. Alas, it has been our destiny to witness the dreadful spectacle of children, women, and old men being treated like vile beasts; of families being torn apart and deported to unknown destinations. ... In our diocese, frightful things are taking place in Noe and Recebedou [camps]. ... The Jews are our brethren. They belong to mankind. No Christian dares forget that![35]

A week later the priests of the diocese of Montauban read to their congregations a letter from their bishop, Pierre-Marie Theas:

> On behalf of my outraged Christian conscience, I raise my voice in protest [against the treatment of Jews], and I assert that all men, Aryans and non-Aryans, are brothers because they have been created by the same God; that all men, whatever their race or religion, have the right to be respected by individuals and states. The present antisemitic pressures flout human dignity and violate the most sacred rights of the human person and family. ...[36]

That Pius' exhortations were effective, and that local officials charged with "the Jewish question" recognized this, there is no doubt. Witness a communication to SS Standard-Leader Dr.

Knochen in early summer of 1943 concerning south-eastern France, then occupied by Italian forces:

> A treasonable propaganda is exploiting this difference between the conceptions of the German and the Italian governments in the matter of solving the Jewish question. Its theme is the following: in the first place, the "worthiness" of the measures applied; and in the second place, their Christian and Catholic conception, as it is inspired by the Vatican.[37]

How receptive the Vatican was to proposals for helping the Jews is illustrated by the story of the now legendary Father Marie-Benoit of Marseilles. Conditions in France had become acutely dangerous for Jews by late 1942; the Vichy government had promised to deliver 50,000 Jews of foreign origin to the Germans, and had begun a ruthless manhunt that summer, especially in the large cities on the Mediterranean coast. Vichy had been allowing Jews to slip into Southeastern France, a free zone, for several years, so that the normal Jewish population of some 15,000 had increased by many ten thousands when Italian forces entered the area on November 11, 1942. Father Marie-Benoit, a Capuchin priest, not only persuaded the Italian inspector-general of police in Nice, Guido Lospinoso, not to comply with the deportation orders, but proceeded — under the perhaps deliberately blind eye of the Italian occupation forces — to turn his monastery in Marseilles into a veritable rescue factory manufacturing passports, identification cards, certificates of baptism, and employers' recommendation letters for Jews, and to smuggle numbers of Jews into Spain and Switzerland. But the priest was not satisfied with these enterprises, and took advantage of a trip to Rome — he had been summoned by the Italian government to be censured for his suspected activities — to present a larger plan to Pius XII on July 16, 1943. In essence, the plan would include gathering information on the where-abouts of Jews deported from France eastward, particularly to Upper Silesia, the location of Auschwitz; obtaining more humane treatment of Jews in French concentration camps; working for the repatriation of Spanish Jews who were residing in France; and transferring some 50,000 French Jews to North Africa where, in view of Allied military successes, they would be safe. The Pope agreed heartily with Father Marie-Benoit's plan, and helped him obtain pledges of support from Britain and the United States as well as from Jewish organization sources in the Allied countries. But the project was destined to fail; with the surrender of the Badoglio government to the Allies, German troops swept into the Italian zone of France, and thousands of Jews fled in panic across the Alps into Italy and Switzerland.

Determined to salvage what he could of his plan, Father Marie-Benoit again approached the Vatican, which helped him prevail upon the Spanish government to authorize its consuls in France to issue entry permits to all Jews who could prove Spanish nationality. In case of doubt, the final decision rested in the hands of that impartial arbiter, Father Marie-Benoit.[38]

In Belgium, the Catholics of Liege observed February 28, 1943, as a day of prayer for the persecuted Jews throughout Europe. Said the Catholic newspaper *Appel des Cloches*, "In communing and praying this Sunday for the persecuted Jewish people who were once Christ's chosen people, we shall be acting in accordance with the directives issued by His Eminence the Bishop."[39]

Pius XII's record in relation to the Jews of Germany, which the Pope knew well from his 12 years there as papal nuncio, is very significant, for from Germany has come the defamatory picture of the wartime pope as a criminal. Numbers of German Christians and Jews have published vehement denials of Hochhuth's charge. They support their position by citing Pius' actions to help the Jews through his representatives in Germany. Msgr. Walter Adolph, Vicar-General of the diocese of Berlin, has written a particularly cogent account. He says that Pius XII, in previously unpublished correspondence with Bishop (later Cardinal) von Preysing of Berlin, encouraged him and his clergy in their protests against every sort of inhumanity. Typical of Pius' letters is this one:

> We are grateful to you, dear Brother, for the clear and open words you have spoken on different occasions to your faithful community and thus to the public; We think hereby of your statement on June 28, 1942, among others, about the Christian conception of right and justice; of your speech on Totensonntag [Sunday of the Dead] last November about the fundamental human right to life and love; We think also especially of your Pastoral, issued on Advent, 1942, and which was also directed to the West German Church Provinces, on God's sovereign rights of the individual and the rights of the family.[40]

We know from Goebbel's diary that the many pastoral letters issued in Germany during the war aroused the Nazis' contempt and hatred.

One of the Pope's letters to Bishop von Preysing treats the central dilemma that faced Pius XII all during the war:

> We leave it to the [local] bishops to weigh the circumstances in deciding whether or not to exercise restraint, *ad maiora mala vitanda* [to avoid greater evil]. This would be advisable if the danger of retaliatory and coercive measures would be imminent in cases of public statements by the bishop. Here lies one of the reasons We Ourselves restrict Our public statements. The experience We had in 1942 with documents which We

released for distribution to the faithful gives justification, as far as We can see, for Our attitude.[41]

The history of Vatican intervention in Nazi cruelties to the Jews dates back to April, 1933, when Pope Pius XI sent an urgent request to the then new Hitler government not to let itself be influenced by antisemitic aims. From 1939 onward, the public record shows countless Vatican intercessions on behalf of Jews, both prompted by pleas from Jewish and other sources and owing to the personal initiative of Pius XII. Many German Catholic prelates met their death as a result of their criticism of the Reich for its treatment of Jews. One, Msgr. Bernhard Lichtenberg, dean of St. Hedwig's Cathedral in Berlin, called on his congregation to pray "for Jews and inmates of concentration camps" after the pograms of November, 1938, and his many similar protests led to his arrest in October, 1942. "We have been comforted to hear . . . that the Catholics, especially the Catholics in Berlin, have extended much love to the so-called non-Aryans, and in this connection We want to say a special word of fatherly appreciation and heartfelt sympathy for Father Lichtenberg, who is imprisoned."[42] Father Lichtenberg voluntarily applied for transfer to the ghetto in Lodz, but was sent to Dachau instead; he died on the way to the camp in November, 1943.[43]

What were Pius XII's actions in Italy, his native land and the country surrounding his own Vatican City? What was his response to the evils being committed almost literally under his windows, since the Jewish ghetto in Rome was so near the Vatican?

Early in the German occupation of Italy, the SS began their persecution of the Jews. On September 27, 1943, one of the commanders demanded of the Jewish community in Rome payment of 100 pounds of gold in 36 hours, failing which 300 Jews would be taken prisoner. The Jewish Community Council worked desperately, but was able to gather together only 70 pounds of the precious metal. In his memoirs, the then Chief Rabbi Zolli of Rome writes that he was sent to the Vatican, where arrangements had already been made to receive him as an "engineer" called to survey a construction problem so that the Gestapo on watch at the Vatican would not bar his entry. He was met by the Vatican treasurer and secretary of state, who told him that the Holy Father himself had given orders for the deficit to be filled with gold vessels taken from the Treasury.[44] There is some disagreement today among some of the principals involved — Zolli, other prominent Jews of Rome, and Father Robert Leiber — over the amount of gold demanded as ransom and whether the Community Council actually borrowed the gold; but there is no question that the Vatican did make the offer.

From the first days of the war, Pope Pius distributed untold sums to aid Jews all over Europe. The Vatican's own refugee agencies and the St. Raphael Verein gave financial and other material help in amounts we cannot begin to guess until the Vatican archives are opened, but the sums which passed through the hands of the Pallottine Fathers, who administered the St. Raphael Verein and who kindly gave me material from their own records, were very large. In addition, Pope Pius supervised the receipt and disposition of funds sent in his care by various sympathetic individuals and groups in Europe and the Americas, notably the Catholic Refugee Committee of the United States. American Jews put large sums into the hands of the Pope, who distributed them according to the wishes of the donors; Father Leiber estimates that Pius received some 2 billion lire from Jews in the United States by the end of 1945.[45]

Pius XII was as sensitive to the spiritual needs of the Jews during World War II as he was to their material wants. None of the many

Vatican services for refugees worked harder at its tasks than the Uffizio Informazioni Vaticano, to which Pius XII assigned the difficult job of seeking news for Jews in Italy of relatives who had been interned or left in other countries. The German Division of the Office of Information received a total of 102,026 appeals for information concerning Jews still in Germany between 1941 and 1945, and was able to furnish 36,877 replies, despite the fact that as the war wore on it could use few standard channels of investigation because of the danger that direct inquiry would have involved for the subjects.

When the Nazis forbade ritual slaughter to the Jews, the Pope sent *shohetim* into Vatican City to perform the ritual slaughter and store food for the Jews sheltered there. Many Jewish citizens, expelled from government, scientific, and teaching positions, were invited to the Vatican; the president and two professors from the University of Rome and a famous geographer, all Jews ousted by the Fascists, received important positions in Vatican City. Bernard Berenson, who preferred to remain in Italy during the war, was given asylum in a villa near Florence, which belonged to the Holy See's minister to the Republic of San Marino, so that he could continue to work and live unmolested; he and his family stayed there, under the flag of the Vatican's diplomatic immunity, until British and American troops arrived in the late summer of 1944.

A Jewish organization, the Delegation for Assistance to Jewish Emigrants (DELASEM), established in Genoa in September, 1939, was forced underground when the Germans occupied the city. Its treasure of 5 million lire was entrusted to Father Giuseppe Repetto, secretary to the archbishop of Genoa; a fifth of this sum was put in the hands of one Padre Benedetto, newly appointed president of DELASEM, who took the money to Rome on April 20, 1944. DELASEM continued its operations from its new headquarters in Father Benedetto's residence, the International College of Capuchins in Rome, and through the indefatigable prelate kept in touch with the International Red Cross, the Pontifical Relief Commission, the Italian police and other civil authorities, and even the German occupation forces. The priest set his coreligionists and DELASEM to work manufacturing false documents and establishing contact with sympathetic Italian, Swiss, Hungarian, French, and Romanian officials.[47] If these details seem familiar, it should come as no surprise; Father Benedetto was the French Father Marie-Benoit, who had gone to Italy when his grand plan to help the Jews in southeastern France collapsed under the German Occupation of the region.

Among the thousands of personal histories of Vatican assistance, moral and material, is that of Dr. Meier Mendes, who recently recalled in a Catholic newspaper the efforts made on behalf of his family in 1939. When Dr. Mendes' father lost his professorship at the University of Rome as a result of the Fascist antisemitic campaigns, the Vatican offered him an important post at a Catholic university in South America. Professor Mendes asked in return whether the Church could help him and his family reach Palestine; the British government, said Dr. Mendes, had restricted immigration severely. Acting on instructions from Pius XII, the then Msgr. Giovanni Battista Montini, pro-secretary of state, "intervened vigorously" with the British authorities and succeeded in obtaining an immigration certificate for the Mendes family outside the regular immigration quotas.[48]

In the realm of material help for refugees, Pius XII's program under the direction of Father Anton Weber was perhaps the broadest in scope of any of the Pope's special aid operations.

Father Weber, today procurator-general of the Order of the Pallotines in Rome, operated a rescue mission during the war for

Nazi victims that was the direct outgrowth of the work Eugenio Cardinal Pacelli, when Vatican secretary of state, had begun on behalf of Jews in 1936. That year the German bishops had requested Cardinal Pacelli to ask the Vatican to found an International Emigrant Organization; Pius XI had agreed, and the Cardinal himself had written to all the American bishops asking for their support.[49]

Prior to Italy's entry into the war, masses of Jews fled to Italy from Germany, Austria, Poland, Hungary, Yugoslavia, and other Balkan states. St. Raphael Verein, an organization long active in helping emigrants leaving Europe for the New World, received instructions from Pope Pius to give the refugees care, without regard to their religion or nationality. Father Weber shortly had a well-run organization working for the protection and help of refugees in every imaginable direction. He first established contact with Jews scattered all over Italy to prepare for possible emigration, and then, with the uninterrupted assistance of the Vatican, tackled the mountain of practical problems facing his enterprise. Passports, visas, medical certificates — valid and otherwise — had to be procured; the papal Ministry of State made innumerable requests of foreign governments for exit and entry papers, with more than fair success. The government of Brazil, for instance, supplied 3000 entry visas at first intended for Jewish converts to Catholicism, but that they were used by practicing Jews is undisputed. Transit visas, many of them for Portuguese ports, were difficult to procure from that country because its government required each emigrant to present a paid steamer ticket first; Father Weber established a special office in Lisbon, which was supported by Vatican funds, to handle that process. The operating costs of the rescue group were enormous; the price for each emigrant — transportation, food, and shelter — could run upward of $800; and the first source for this money was the Vatican itself. By 1945 Father Weber's organization had given assistance to some 25,000 Jews, 4000 of whom were able to travel to safety overseas.[50]

I used the phrase "valid and otherwise" regarding the official papers Father Weber's organization procured for Jews. The cloak-and-dagger story of the false documents supplied to Jews by the Church all over Europe and the Near East is not yet fully known; nor, if it were, could it be told, for there are countless numbers of Jews whose peaceful enjoyment of their new citizenship today still depends on the apparent validity of these papers. The Vatican both initiated and lent its support to a remarkable variety of secret manufacturing enterprises — like that of Father Marie-Benoit in France and later in Italy — as well as exerted pressure on Allied and neutral governments to grant entry or at least transit to Jews in danger of their lives. Jewish refugees in France holding Paraguayan passports in 1943 and 1944 approached the Vatican for help, fearing that recognition of their papers would be withdrawn by that South American government; through the apostolic delegate in Paraguay, the Pope obtained assurances that the passports would continue to be valid. The Vatican interceded with the Germans to allow Jews in Bergen Belsen who held South American passports to receive packages of food and clothing. Endless other examples could be cited, but perhaps the most extraordinary part of this particular rescue mission is what Ira Hirschmann has called Operation Baptism.

Archbishop Cassulo's 1941 protest in Romania was in answer to a state ruling that a change of religious status by a Jew did not alter his legal status as a member of that persecuted "race." For the authorities had become suspicious, as did those in the Balkans, Hungary, and elsewhere later, of the number of Jewish "converts" to Catholicism. Until such a ruling was made in a Nazi-controlled country, however, a Jew who could prove himself a member of the Catholic Church could usually use the evidence of that membership-a baptismal certificate — as a safe-conduct paper to leave the country. No records have been published regarding who conceived the idea or how it was implemented, but the existence of the false baptismal certificates, and they number in the thousands, is a fact. It is also a fact that the Vatican was well aware of the plan, and that members of resistance groups, apostolic nuncios, nuns, representatives of Jewish aid groups based in the Allied countries, and untold numbers of ordinary citizens risked their welfare if not their lives to promote the ingenious scheme. By mid-1944, when only the Jews of Budapest had been temporarily spared in blood-soaked Hungary, another beloved Catholic figure had thrown his weight to the wheel, increasing the distribution of the baptismal certificates many times over; this was Pius XII's close friend and successor, Archbishop Roncalli, the late Pope John XXIII.[51]

With the arrival of the Germans in Italy, the Jewish population was threatened by the same sword that had ruthlessly cut down so many of their coreligionists in other parts of Europe. The Pope spoke out strongly in their defense with the first mass arrests of Jews in 1943, and *L'Osservatore Romano* carried an article protesting the internment of Jews and the confiscation of their property. The Fascist press came to call the Vatican paper "a mouthpiece of the Jews," echoing the April, 1941 denunciation of the publication by Roberto Farinacci, Italy's leading promoter of racist doctrines.[52] In keeping with Pius' conviction that direct attack on Fascist policies would cause more harm than good, the Vatican paper had curbed its criticism of the regime after Italy's entry into the war, but it continued to carry statements like that made in March, 1943, that no social order "could be based on racial privilege and force."[53]

The emigration operations in Italy necessarily came to a halt, with the last plane carrying Jewish refugees leaving Rome on September 8, 1943, and Father Weber's St. Raphael Verein turned to the dangerous task of assigning the Jews left behind to hiding places. The Pope sent out the order that religious buildings were to give refuge to Jews, even at the price of great personal sacrifice on the part of their occupants; he released monasteries and convents from the cloister rule forbidding entry into these religious houses to all but a few specified outsiders, so that they could be used as hiding places. Thousands of Jews — the figures run from 4000 to 7000 — were hidden, fed, clothed, and bedded in the 180 known places of refuge in Vatican City, churches and basilicas, Church administrative buildings, and parish houses. Unknown numbers of Jews were sheltered in Castel Gandolfo, the site of the Pope's summer residence, private homes, hospitals, and nursing institutions; and the Pope took personal responsibility for the care of the children of Jews deported from Italy.

During the whole period of mass hiding of Jews, the Germans made only two raids and captured only a handful of people. The Pope protested strongly, and no further raids occurred; further, though the sheltered groups included many non-Jewish refugees, there was not a single case of betrayal.[54]

One hiding place for Jews was a Jesuit church with a false ceiling. Each man given refuge in the church was assigned to a space over a side altar and referred to by the name of the saint which the altar carried. The priests of the church delighted in chatting about "Zavier" and "Robert Bellarmine" and "Gonzaga" in the presence of Nazi officers, who never caught on to the game.[55]

The mass media have filled us with the sickening count of the lives sacrificed by the Nazis to their theory of racial purity; what we do not know is how many lives were saved by the humane work of such men as Pius XII. Official figures, cold as they are, may give us an inkling. In 1939 there were some 50,000 Jews in Italy;

in 1946, there 46,000, of whom 30,000 were Italians and 16,000 refugees from Germany, Poland, Hungary, Yugoslavia, France, and other countries. Approximately 8000 Jews in all were taken by the Gestapo[56] — a horrifying cipher, like all such, but far smaller than those that follow the names of most Nazi-occupied or -controlled countries in the roll call of genocidal slaughter.

Ten years after his address to the pilgrims at Lourdes, Pope Pius returned full circle to the theme of brotherhood which, contrary to playwright Hochhuth's allegations, inspired his unflagging help to persecuted Jews. After the liberation of Rome, while there was apprehension over the fate of Jewish prisoners in the hands of the Axis powers in northern Italy and Germany, he said: "For centuries the Jews have been most unjustly treated and despised. It is time they were treated with justice and humanity. God wills it and the Church wills it. St. Paul tells us that the Jews are our brothers. Instead of being treated as strangers, they should be welcomed as friends."[57]

The tangible evidence of Pius' real character — his love for all men, and his particular concern for "justice and humanity" toward Jews — lies in the fact that throughout the war Jewish leaders from all over the globe approached him for help. One of the foremost of these was Chief Rabbi Isaac Herzog of Jerusalem, to whom the Pope gave the message that he would do everything in his power to help the persecuted Jews. Rabbi Herzog traveled to Constantinople to seek financial and other assistance for his Jewish Aid Fund, and, true to the Pope's word, found in the apostolic delegate in Istanbul, Archbishop Angelo Roncalli, an uncommonly dynamic collaborator in the rescue operations carried out for the Balkan Jews.[58] A letter dated February 28, 1944, which the future John XXIII wrote the Vatican to transmit a plea from Rabbi Herzog for help for the Jews of Romania, began: "Chief Rabbi Herzog of Jerusalem . . . came to the Apostolic Delegation personally in order to thank the Holy Father and the Holy See officially for the many forms of charity extended to Jews in these last years . . . ."[59]

After the war Rabbi Herzog sent "a special blessing" to the Pope for "his lifesaving efforts on behalf of the Jews during the Nazi occupation of Italy," through the intermediary of Harry Greenstein, now executive director of the Associated Jewish Charities of Baltimore. Mr. Greenstein said in a recent interview, "I still remember quite vividly the glow in his eyes. He replied that his only regret was that he was not able to save many more Jews."[60]

This is but one of the thousands of voices that have praised Pope Pius XII's great work on behalf of the Jewish people. Let me pick a few more at random.

On June 4, 1944, when the Allies entered Rome, the *Jewish News Bulletin* of the British 8th Army said: "To the everlasting credit of the people of Rome, and the Roman Catholic Church, the lot of the Jews has been made easier by their truly Christian offers of assistance and shelter. Even now, many still remain in places which opened their doors to hide them from the fate of deportation to certain death . . . . The full story of the help given to our people by the Church cannot be told, for obvious reasons, until after the war." At a meeting of the National Committee of Liberation, a Jewish speaker said: "It was in the name of the frankest feeling of brotherhood that the Church did its utmost to rescue our threatened people from destruction. The supreme ecclesiastical authorities and all those priests who suffered for us in imprisonment and in concentration camps have our eternal gratitude."[61] A prominent Jewish citizen of Rome declared: "Our Catholic brothers have done more for us than we can ever do to repay." Rabbi Elio Toaff, now Chief Rabbi of Rome, said after the death of the Pope: " More than anyone else, we have had the opportunity to appreciate the great kindness, filled with compassion and magnanimity, that the Pope displayed during the terrible years of persecution and terror, when it seemed that there was no hope left for us."[62] And Rabbi Zolli wrote: "What the Vatican did will be indelibly and eternally engraved in our hearts . . . . Priests and even high prelates did things that will forever be an honor to Catholicism."[63] No less grateful were the words uttered on Pius' death by the chief rabbis of Egypt, London, and France. At the United Nations, Israel's Minister of Foreign Affairs, Mrs. Golda Meier, said:

> We share the grief of the world over the death of His Holiness Pius XII. During a generation of wars and dissensions, he affirmed the high ideals of peace and compassion. During the ten years of Nazi terror, when our people went through the horrors of martyrdom, the Pope raised his voice to condemn the persecutors and to commiserate with their victims. The life of our time has been enriched by a voice which expressed the great moral truths above the tumults of daily conflicts. We grieve over the loss of a great defender of peace.[64]

Dr. Nahum Goldmann, president of the World Jewish Congress, wrote in his letter of condolence on Pope Pius' death: "With special gratitude we remember all he has done for the persecuted Jews during one of the darkest periods in their entire history." In 1945, the Congress had made a gift of $20,000 to Vatican charities in recognition of the work of the Holy See in rescuing Jews from Fascist persecution; and an interoffice memorandum, written a year earlier by a WJC official closely involved in the Congress' pleas to Pius XII for help for the Jews of Poland, reads: "The

Catholic Church in Europe has been extraordinarily helpful to us in a multitude of ways. From Hinsley in London to Pacelli in Rome, to say nothing of the anonymous priests in Holland, France, and elsewhere, they have done very notable things for us . . . . „65

On April 7, 1944, Rabbi Safran of Bucharest paid tribute to the Catholic Church's activities on behalf of Romanian Jews in a letter to the papal nuncio:

> Excellency:
>
> In these harsh times our thoughts turn more than ever with respectful gratitude to what has been accom-plished by the Sovereign Pontiff on behalf of Jews in general and by Your Excellency on behalf of the Jews of Romania and Transnistria.
>
> In the most difficult hours which we Jews of Romania have passed through, the generous assistance of the Holy See, carried out by the intermediary of your high person, was decisive and salutary. It is not easy for us to find the right words to express the warmth and consolation we experienced because of the concern of the supreme Pontiff, who offered a large sum to relieve the sufferings of deported Jews, sufferings which had been pointed out to him by you after your visit to Transnistria. The Jews of Romania will never forget these facts of historic importance . . . [66]

Some of the voices which eulogized Pius XII five or twenty years ago remain silent in the face of Rolf Hochhuth's allegations; a few have agreed with him. Why is this? Were men wrong then, or are they wrong now? Are some of the Catholics of Europe, who should be forever grateful to Pope Pius for not putting them to the agonizing choice between country and church, perhaps relieved to see blame heaped on another head?

No one who reads the record of Pius XII's actions on behalf of Jews can subscribe to Hochhuth's accusation. However, though the evidence moves against the hypothesis that a formal condemnation from Pius would have curtailed the mass murder of Jews, this is still a question of judgment. Two men present the complexities of that question very succinctly., One, Leon Poliakov, wrote the following sentence in *Commentary* in November, 1950:

> It is painful to have to state that at a time when gas chambers and crematoria were operating day and night, the high spiritual authority of the Vatican did not find it necessary to make a clear and solemn protest that would have echoed through the world; and yet one cannot say that there may not have been pertinent and valid reasons for this silence.

The second speaker is the new Holy Father, Pope Paul VI, whose letter, quoted in part below, reached the offices of *The Tablet* in London an hour after his election to the papacy, and was published in the issue of June 29:

> It is not my intention here to examine the question raised ... [in] the play *Der Stellvertreter*: namely, whether it was Pius XII's duty to condemn in some public and spectacular way the massacres of the Jews during the last war ....

> For my part I conceive it my duty to contribute to the task of clarifying and unifying men's judgment on the

historical reality in question — so distorted in the representational pseudoreality of Hochhuth's play . . . .

[Pius XII] wished to enter fully into the history of his own afflicted time; with a deep sense that he himself was a part of that history, he wished to participate fully in it, to share its sufferings in his own heart and soul. Let me cite, in this connexion, the words of a well-qualified witness, Sir D'Arcy Osborne, the British Minister to the Holy See who, when the Germans occupied Rome, was obliged to live confined in the Vatican City. Writing to *The Times* on May 20th, Sir D'Arcy said: "Pius XII was the most warmly humane, kindly, generous, sympathetic (and, incidentally, saintly) character that it has been my privilege to meet in the course of a long life."
. . .

Let some men say what they will, Pius XII's reputation as a true Vicar of Christ, as one who tried, so far as he could, fully and courageously to carry out the mission entrusted to him, will not be affected . . . .

Notes

Editor's Note: These notes are reproduced exactly as given in the original 1963 edition. There have been some changes in footnote style and usage in the intervening years,but we did not feel that these changes warranted a reworking of these notes.

1 Quoted in Sir Alec Randall, "The Pope, the Jews, and the Nazis" (pamphlet), London, Catholic Truth Society, 1963,p. 18; see also in Peter White, "An Attack on Pope Pius XII," *Jubilee,* June, 1963.

2 Quoted in White, op. cit.; see also Paul Duclos, *Le Vatican et la seconde guerre mondial,* Paris, Pedone,1955, pp. 221-223.

3 Quoted by Dr. Robert M. W. Kempner in *Frankfurter Allgemeine Zeitung,* May 23, 1963.

4 Angelo Martini, S.J., *"II Vacario:* Unatragedia cristiana?" (reprint) *Civilta Cattolica,*1963, II (2710), 324.

5 Angelo Martini, S.J., "La Santa Sede e gli ebreidella Romania durante la seconda guerra mondiale" (reprint),*Civilta Cattolica,* 1951, III (2669), 459.

6 Quoted in Martini, *"Il Vicario...,* p. 317.

7 Sir D'Arcy Osborne, a Protestant, was the British Minister to the Vatican during World War II; Msgr. Giovannettiand Father Leiber, both Catholics, are respectively a member of the Vatican's Congregation for Extraordinary Ecclesiastical Affairs and the former Secretary to Pope Pius; Harry Greenstein,a Jew, is the executive director of the Associated Jewish Charities of Baltimore.

8 Randall, *op. cit.,* p. 19.

9 Quoted in Robert Leiber, S.J., "Pio XII e gli ebreidi Roma, 1943-1944" (reprint), *Civilta Cattolica,*1961, I (2675), 455.

10In the German edition; in the English edition (tr. Robert David Macdonald, London, Methuen, 1963), the "Historical Sidelights" run 63 pages.

11*The Representative* (English ed.), p. viii. The source for the Mauriac quotation is the preface he wrote for Poliakov's *Breviaire de la haine,* Paris, Calmann-Levy,1951.

12Leon Poliakov, "Le Vatican et la question juive,"*Monde juif,* December, 1950; quoted in Duclos, op. cit.,j pp. 191-192.

13Poliakov, *Breviare de la haine*; quoted in Leiber,op. cit., p. 457.

14Published in *Monde juif,* June, 1949; quoted in Duclos, *op. cit.,* p. 222, and in Leiber, op. cit., pp.449-450.

15Quoted in *Frankfurter Allgemeine Zeitung,* March 4,1963.

16Quoted in Duclos, *op. cit.,* p. 185.

17Quoted in *Frankfurter Allgemeine Zeitung,* March 4,1963.

18Quoted in Fiorello Cavalli, S.J., "La Santa Sede contro le deportazioni degli ebrei dalla Slovacchia durante la seconda guerra mondiale" (reprint), *Civilta Cattolica,*1961, III (2665), 7; and in Jozef Lettrich, *History of Modern Slovakia,* New York, Praeger, 1955, p. 187.

19Quoted in Cavalli, *op. cit.,* p. 8n.

20Quoted in *Ibid.,* p. 13.

21Quoted in *Ibid.,* p. 17.

22Martini, "La Santa Sede...," p. 454. The February 16 intervention was on behalf of Jewish converts to Catholicism; thereafter, the Archbishop worked for all Jews.

23Deposition of Rabbi Safran introduced by Gabriel Bach into the record of the Eichmann trial, at Decision No. 46; and Martini, "La Santa Sede...," p. 460.

24Quoted in Martini, "La Santa Sede...," p. 449.

25Poliakov, "Le Vatican. . ."; quoted in Duclos,*op. cit.*, p. 192.

26Martini, "La Santa Sede...," p. 459.

27Document No. CXLV, a-60, Archives of the Centre de Documentation juive, Paris; quoted in Philip Friedman, *Their Brothers' Keepers,* New York, Crown, 1957, p. 212.

28Gerhard Reitlinger, *The Final Solution,* New York, Beechhurst Press, 1953, p. 431.

29World Jewish Congress memorandum, "The Vatican and the Jews," dated March 24, 1959 (photostat).

30*Ibid.*

31Quoted in Friedman, *op. cit.*, p. 87; see also pp.84-86.

32Quoted in *American Jewish Yearbook*, 1942-1943, Philadelphia, Jewish Publication Society, p. 215.

33Friedman, *op. cit.,* p. 194.

34Quoted in*American Jewish Yearbook, 1943-1944,*Philadelphia, Jewish Publication Society, p. 292.

35Quoted in John M. Oesterreicher, *Racisme--Antisemitisme--Antichristianisme,* New York, Maison Francaise, 1943, pp. 239-240; see New York Times,September 9, 1942.

36Quoted in*American Jewish Yearbook, 1945-1946,*Philadelphia, Jewish Publication Society, p. 117.

37Quoted in Leon Poliakov and Jacques Sabile, *Jews Under the Italian Occupation,* Paris, Editions du Centre, 1955,p. 96.

38See, among many other sources, *ibid.,* pp. 40n, 21-23; Friedman, *op cit.,* pp. 55-58; Duclos, *op.cit.,* p. 189.

39Quoted in *American Jewish Yearbook, 1943-1944,* p.263.

40Quoted in Father Walter Adolph, "Hochhuths fanatisches Voruteil," *Deutsche Tagespost,* March 12,1963.

41Quoted in *Tablet* (London), March 16, 1963.

42Quoted in Adolph, *op. cit.*

43*See,* e.g., Friedman. *op. cit.,* pp. 94-95.*The Representative* is dedicated to Father Lichtenberg and Father Maximilian Kolbe, the latter an internee at Auschwitz.

44Eugenio Maria Zolli (Israele Anton Zoller). *Before the Dawn: Autobiographical Reflections,* New York, Sheed &Ward, 1954, pp. 159-161.

45Leiber, *op. cit.,* p. 452.

46*Ibid.,* p. 453.

47 See, *ibid.,* p. 452; *Jewish Advocate* (Boston), May 4, 1963; Poliakov and Sabille, *op. cit.,* p.j 40n.

48*Catholic News,* July 11, 1963, sec. C.5, p. 2.

49*Rheinische Post*, September 9, 1961.

50*Ibid.*; and *Boston Globe,* January 27, 1963.

51On false Catholic papers, see, e.g., Ira Hirschmann,*Caution to the Winds,* New York, McKay, 1962. pp. 179-185.

52*American Jewish Yearbook, 1940-1941,* Philadelphia,Jewish Publication Society, pp. 384-385; *Osservatore Romano,* January 29, 1961.

53*American Jewish Yearbook, 1943-1944,* p. 292.

54_The Tidings,_ June 9, 1961; World Jewish Congress memorandum dated March 24, 1959; Leiber, op. cit., p. 451;_American Jewish Yearbook, 1944-1945,_ Philadelphia, Jewish Publication Society, 1944, pp. 233-234; Zolli, op. cit., 187-188.

55_Evening Union Leader_, June 29, 1963.

56Leiber, _op. cit.,_ p. 450.

57See Joseph L. Lichten, "Pope Pius XII and the Jews" (reprint), _ADL Bulletin,_ October, 1958.

58Tablet (Brooklyn), March 21, 1963.

59Quoted in Martini, "La Santa Sede...," p. 461.

60_Tablet_ (Brooklyn), March 21, 1963.

61_See_ Lichten, _op. cit._

62Quoted in _Frankfurter Allgemeine Zeitung,_ March 4,1963.

63Quoted in _American Jewish Yearbook, 1944-1945,_ p.233.

64Quoted in _Civilta Cattolica,_ 1958, III, 323.

65World Jewish Congress memorandum dated March 24, 1959.

66Quoted in Martini, "La Santa Sede...," p. 462.

APPENDICES

THE
PRIESTS
OF
DACHAU

Rev. William J. O'Malley, S.J., teaches theology and English at Fordham Preparatory School, Bronx, N.Y. He is currently seeking a publisher for three novels he has written about the priests of Dachau. This article, which appeared originally in the Nov. 14, 1987 issue of *America* magazine, is based on his research for those novels. It is included in this reader because it so forcefully demonstrates the enormous scope of the anti-Catholic aspect of the Holocaust. It is reprinted by permission of the author and of America Press, Inc., 106 West 56th Street, New York, NY 10019.

Appendix A

The Priests of Dachau

by William J. O'Malley, S.J.

For five years, Konzentrationslager Dachau, a short bicycle ride across the sodden moors northwest of Munich, was the site of the largest religious community in the world. Because many records were hurriedly burned as the American tanks approached in April 1945, the best estimate, based on clandestine lists kept by priest-prisoners in the work offices, is that 2,771 clergymen were interned at KZ Dachau — of whom at least 1,034 died in the camp. The 2,579 Catholic priests, lay brothers and seminarians came from 38 nations, from 134 dioceses and 29 religious orders and congregations. Their community included 109 Protestant, 30 Orthodox and two Moslem clergymen.

That figure, surprising as it might be, does not include the clergy or nuns shot or beheaded or tortured to death in squares and alleys and jails all over Europe. In the first 16 months of the war, 700 Polish priests died at the hands of the Nazis and 3,000 more were sent to concentration camps; more than half did not return. In Dachau, 868 Polish priests perished--300 of them in medical experiments or by torture in the prison showers. In France, too, by February 1944, the Gestapo had arrested 162 priests, of whom 123 were shot or decapitated before ever reaching any camp. According to the International Tribunal at Nuremburg, 780 priests died of exhaustion at Mauthausen and 300 at Sachsenhausen, and there were hundreds of other camps and satellites in the network. Nor does the total figure of 2,771 take into consideration that one-quarter to one-third of those shipped to any camp often arrived dead.

The Polish clergy in Dachau (1,780) far outnumbered the others. They arrived first, and most of the 830 who survived did so, unbelievably, for five years. As for the Czech and Slovak priests (109) and the Yugoslavs (50), the reason for incarceration was, as with the Jews, racial. Hitler believed Slavs were ordained by Providence to be slaves to the Aryan race, a fact their very name "proved." Any Slav who had achieved an education had, by that fact, flown in the face of his own nature. Moreover, these priests were not only educated Slavs but apostles of a church that Hitler had vowed to "crush like a toad" when final victory arrived.

The German and Austrian clergy at Dachau (447) were for the most part men who realized that being a good Christian and a good Nazi were as irreconcilable as compassion and sadism. These men, being celibate, were freer than family men to take risks. They had run underground presses and underground railways to rescue retarded children from the euthanasia laws and Jews from deportation. Any priest was free to defy the Pulpit Law and speak out against the racism and paganism of the Third Reich, but — except for the redoubtable Bishop Von Galen of Muenster — it would be his final public word. German priests and pastors were exiled to Dachau for preaching love of neighbor, for insisting that Jesus was a Jew, for warning S.S. men that they could not abjure their faith to achieve promotion, for offering requiem Masses even for relatives of Communists. German religious were interned on trumped-up-charges of spiriting funds out of the country to their headquarters in Rome and, in much publicized cases, for seducing boys and girls. Two old priests were sent to Dachau for failing to give the Hitler salute when Hermann Goering and his entourage entered a Berlin restaurant. All the Gestapo needed was to present a paper to any priest: "Evidence confirmed by the State police shows that by his behavior he is endangering the stability and security of the State."

The 156 French, 63 Dutch, and 46 Belgians were primarily interned for their work in the Underground. If that were a crime, such men as Michel Riquet, S.J., surely had little defense; he was in contact with most of the leaders of the French Resistance and was their chaplain, writing forthright editorials for the underground press, sequestering Jews, POW's, downed Allied airmen, feeding and clothing them, providing them with counterfeit papers and spiriting them into Spain and North Africa. Henry Zwaans, a Jesuit secondary school teacher in The Hague, was arrested for distributing copies of Bishop Von Galen's homilies and died in Dachau of dropsy and dysentery. Jacques Magnee punished a boy for bringing anti-British propaganda into the Jesuit secondary school at Charleroi in Belgium; Leo DeConinck went to Dachau for instructing the Belgian clergy in retreat conferences to resist the Nazis. Parish priests were arrested for quoting Pius XI's anti-Nazi encyclical, *Mit Brennender Sorge*, or for publicly condemning the anti-Semitic film, "The Jew Seuss," or for providing Jews with false baptismal certificates. Some French priests at Dachau disguised themselves as workers to minister to young Frenchmen shanghaied into service in German heavy industry and had been caught doing what they had been ordained to do.

There is little need to rehearse the conditions of their lives in the camp. It was a hell before which Dante would stand mute. A good day was one on which you'd been beaten to your knees only once or twice; one small wad of bread and a cup of watery soup; 12 hours of hard labor, dragging the corpses to the roll call each morning and evening; warehoused at night in tiers, sleeping three to each lice-infested bunk; lugging one's soul from place to place in the fellowship of zombies; the cold, the filth, the endless degrading "hazing," the typhus, the inhuman joy when your best friend was beaten senseless and you were ignored. For some, hell lasted five years of days.

In 1940, it seemed a diplomatic coup that the German bishops and the Vatican had persuaded Heinrich Himmler to concentrate all priests from the network of European camps into one camp, to house them in separate blocks together, with lighter work and a chapel. In early December 1940, priests already interned in Dachau were put into Barracks 26, 28 and 30 at the end of the west side of the long camp street, "Liberty St." Within two weeks they were joined by 800-900 more from Buchenwald, Mauthausen, Auschwitz and other camps, a Babel of haggard strangers. With the conquest of Western Europe, arrests of priests increased so that, now concentrated into two barracks instead of three, despite the deaths, they were rarely fewer than 1,500 men in beds and toilet facilities built for 360. Hardly any priests remained in the other camps.

Priests from Dachau worked in the "Plantation" and in the enormous S.S. industrial complex immediately to the west of the camp. In February 1942, two groups of younger Polish priests and scholastics were chosen for work as carpenters' apprentices, but they had actually been chosen (at the express order of Heinrich Himmler) to be injected with pus to study gangrene or to have their body temperature lowered to 27 degrees Centigrade in order to study resuscitation of German fliers downed in the North Atlantic. The Rev. Andreas Reiser, a German, was crowned with barbed wire and a group of Jewish prisoners was forced to hail him as their king, and the Rev. Stanislaus Bednarski, a Pole, was hanged on a cross.

Although a few priests did throw themselves in despair on the electrified wire and a few did sink into the affectless, zombie Nirvana the prisoners called "going Muslim," most clung to a faith that kept them plodding on. They had been schooled to a charity that was often strained, even with their fellow clergy, by national and ethnic differences. They could communicate at least in Latin across language barriers that divided other prisoners. They were educated men used to using their wits and to taking charge. In early 1943, when the tide of the war began to turn against Germany, and the need to get all the labor possible out of the slaves became clear to the camp commander, the S.S. saw that it was better to have disciplined, educated secretaries and managers. This allowed priests into offices where they could manipulate labor schedules, into the hospital where they could minister to the sick, especially during the two horrifying typhus winters, into the package depot where they made sure that packages (now allowed to ease the food shortage) got to the most needy, especially the Russians who obviously had no packages at all, and into the munitions factories where they could work minor sabotage, particularly with the planned gas oven at Dachau — which never became functional due, at least in part, to their efforts.

But most important to them, they had their chapel. At first, it was a single empty room with two tables shoved together for an altar and the contents of two army chaplains' Mass kits for vestments and vessels. In five years they managed to jerry-rig, "liberate" and sneak in through the Plantation roadstand the elements of a quite creditable chapel. It was to focus their minds and raise their spirits. And when eight months after the chapel opened, the Polish priests were moved to another barrack and forbidden entrance, hosts and wine were spirited to them; from both barracks, the Eucharist spread throughout the camp in tins that had held aspirin and zinc ointment and tobacco. Their greatest triumph, in December of 1944, was the ordination as priest of a young deacon of the diocese of Muenster, Karl Leisner, by his fellow-prisoner, Bishop Gabriel Piquet of Clermont-Ferrand—with full vestments made from material "liberated" from the stores, even a biretta for the ordained, a miter and red shoes for the bishop and a ring and pectoral cross made by a Communist inmate in the Messerschmitt works at Allach—and the S.S. never found out.

The most admirable priest-rogue was a Jesuit former master of novices named Otto Pies. Released from Dachau in the Spring of 1945 as the Americans were advancing, he disguised himself as an S.S. officer and came back to the camp with a truckload of food—rousted God knows where in those bitterly foodless days. He drove into the camp, into the priests' wired-off compound, and then drove off with 30 of the priests hidden in the back. Two days later, when 5,400 prisoners—88 of them priests—were led off into the Alps to be lost in the snow, Otto Pies came back in the same uniform and truck and picked up more.

For such men, Mass was neither duty nor routine. Father Riquet describes a "Mass" he offered at Mauthausen before being moved to Dachau. They had no wine, but in the corner of a barrack, a dozen men squatted in rags as Riquet read the Epistle and Gospel of the day, recited the Our Father and gave them his blessing. At the end, with tears in his eyes, M. Jaspar, the consul general of Belgium, whispered: "That was the most beautiful Mass of my life."

It is important to keep these men's memory alive. As far as I know, there are no Auschwitzes today. But there is a shaming archipelago of Dachaus still—in the Soviet Union and Eastern Europe, in South and Central America, in North and South Africa. We cannot say, "We never knew they were there." Although policy makers have many problems of the moment, the

Jews have been admirably obstreperous — and successful — in their concern for the tragedy of interned Soviet Jews. What of the others? I hear the voice of the Common Man in "A Man for All Seasons," playing Thomas More's jailer: "You've got to understand, sir. I'm just a plain, simple man." More groans in despair, "Sweet Jesus! These plain, simple men!"

PRIESTS
OF THE
HOLOCAUST

Rev. William J. O'Malley, S.J. (the author of **Appendix A,** *The Priests of Dachau*) wrote this piece for *Columbia* magazine's May, 1988 issue which featured several articles centered on the theme "Pius XII and the Holocaust." It is reprinted here with the permission of the author.

Appendix B

Priests of the Holocaust

by William J. O'Malley, S.J.

Somehow the Nazi genocide associated with the word 'Holocaust' focuses primarily on those who died in extermination camps.

If the word "genocide" means the deliberate extermination of a national or racial group, the six million tragic Jewish victims surely qualify. However, so do the nine to ten million Slavic victims who were eliminated — not in the war, not as saboteurs, not as guerrillas, but solely because they were Slavic. One might also argue the case of the half million gypsies and perhaps even the thousands of homosexuals executed because they were not the virile Aryans Hitler considered the only members of the true human race.

Hitler believed Providence intended Slavs to be serfs to the godlike Aryans; after all, medieval Latinists had used the word *sclavus* for both slaves and Slavs. Thus all educated Slavs, especially members of a clergy Hitler had vowed to "crush like a toad" after the war, were to be liquidated — by a year or two of humbling starvation and slavery. As Martin Bormann put it: "All Polish intelligentsia must be exterminated. This sounds cruel, but such is the law of life. . . .(Polish priests) will preach what we want them

The Priests of Dachau

Nationality	No. of priests	Released from camp	Died in camp	Trans-ferred	Survived the War
Polish	1,780	78	868	4	830
German	447	208	94	100	45
French	156	5	10	4	137
Czech/Slovak	109	1	24	10	74
Dutch	63	10	17	–	36
Yugoslav	50	2	4	6	38
Belgian	46	1	9	3	33
Italian	28	–	1	1	26
Luxemburger	16	2	6	–	8
10 other	25	7	1	4	13
	2,720	314	1,034	132	1,240

to preach. If any priest acts differently, we will make short work of him. The task of the priest is to keep the Poles quiet, stupid, and dull-witted."

Ten thousand Poles were liquidated in the first four months of the occupation. Seven hundred Polish priests were shot, and 3,000 were sent to camps, where 2,600 of them died. The majority perished slowly and methodically from medical experiments and starvation labor — compared to which a quick, horrible death in a gas chamber might have seemed a perverse kind of mercy.

In the first week of December, 1940, the SS consolidated the 1,197 priests from all the concentration and execution camps in Europe into a single camp: Dachau — where they could be tightly controlled. They were housed in two barracks, 26 and 28, ringed with a barbed-wire fence — a camp within the camp — so they would be less able to act as priests during their few free hours. By the day of liberation, 2,720 priests, brothers, and seminarians from 134 dioceses and 29 religious orders had dragged out their lives in Konzentrationzlager Dachau. Over 1,000 died there.

These numbers do not, of course, include priests executed in their towns and cities; of 162 French priests arrested by the Gestapo in February, 1944, for instance, 123 were shot or guillotined before reaching any camp. Nor does it count those priests who lived and died in other camps; the International Tribunal at Nuremburg said that 780 priests died of exhaustion in the quarries of KZ Mauthausen alone. Nor does it consider that one-quarter to one-third of those shipped to any camp were often dead on arrival.

The Poles, Czechs, Slovaks, and Yugoslavs, of course, were killed for the same satanic reason as the Jews: race, coupled with achieving an education and association with a Jewish-founded

The Value of a Prisoner to the Reich

(All values shown in Reich Marks)

Daily rental of prisoner to war-related industry....... + 6.00

Deduction for food .... − .60

Deduction for clothes.. − .10

Net value of prisoner *per day* .... + 5.30

Multiplied by average prisoner lifespan (270 days).. *x 270*

Total income generated by prisoner 1,431.00

Additional proceeds from "rational disposal"
(fillings, clothes, bones, valuables, etc.) 200.00

Less cost of cremation.. − 2.00

Value of average prisoner's life 1,629.00

Christianity which Hitler despised for its attempts to effeminize Aryan males with doctrines of mercy and love.

Those from the occupied countries had run escape routes for downed Allied airmen, published underground newspapers, disguised Jews as nuns, seminarians, and Christian orphans, issued false baptismal certificates. Abbe Maury of Nancy was arrested because the Gestapo had found his notice in every French concentration camp: "If ever you are in need of a Good Samaritan, here is my address."

For German priests, refusal to bow to the Third Reich was not only resistance but treason, especially during the war. With the complete suppression of the Catholic press, priests went underground, duplicating the sermons of the redoubtable Bishop von Galen of Muenster exhorting the people to resist the pagan racism of the Nazi regime. Any priest was free to defy the Pulpit Law, but it would be his final public word. As the figures above attest, several hundred German and Austrian priests took that risk — contrary to the view held even by eminent historians that the German Church was embarrassingly, shamefully silent.

Dachau opened in 1933, and its first inmates were Communists, criminals, and other "enemies of the state." Consequently, when the priests arrived, these toughs were by then the trusties of the camp, in sadistic charge of the barracks and the work crews. Every morning at 4:30, the Kapos rousted the prisoners from their bunks where they slept from three to five men on a shelf two-and-a-half-feet wide, for a quick wash — about 275 men at sinks and latrines intended for 50 prisoners, a tepid cup of ersatz coffee, and thence to the endless roll call. Until midway through the war, even the corpses had to be present.

From roll call, prisoners trudged off to the enormous plantation to the east of the camp and to the SS industrial complex to the west of it. In winter, they removed every speck of snow, even from roofs; if there were not enough shovels, they reversed their thin zebra-striped jackets as scoops; they slept in the cold, wet clothes, since each man had only one uniform.

As the war turned and manpower became crucial, the commandant seconded prisoners to nearby industries. BMW in Allach, for instance, employed 3,800 Dachau prisoners, and four Messerschmidt factories accounted for 5,600 more. Manpower meant Reich Marks.

Around noon, watery soup and in the evening thin soup and a wad of bread which the prisoner could wolf down or save to becalm his hunger pains long enough to get to sleep — dangerous, however, since bread was the principal currency of the camp. All prisoners were emaciated down to about one-third their former weight.

Punishment was frequent, often for no observable reason. As one Dachau commandant said, "Softies belong in a monastery, not in the SS." With priests, Jews, and Russians, the SS could do anything, absolutely anything. One young SS man took a great interest in Father Andreas Rieser, who seemed incapable of being broken. One day, after beating Rieser through the camp, the SS man stopped by a group of old Jews dismantling rusted barbed wire entanglements. He looked at the bruised, sweating priest and laughed, "You look like Christ!" he howled, and picked up a length of barbed wire and began whipping Rieser with it. "Braid yourself a crown," he snapped. The young trooper hammered the crown onto the priest's head and forced the old Jews to spit on him. "That's how you treated Christ," he laughed. "A stinking Jew, just like you."

Old-time prisoners convinced newcomers to go without their glasses, since most of the camp personnel had no time for intellectuals, especially for priests. Guards and Kapos carried truncheons and used them gratuitously. Tower guards had orders to shoot any prisoner too near the fence, out of line, speaking during roll call, or within three feet of an SS man.

The principal means of serious punishment was the Bock, a table to which the prisoner was tied while 25 or "twice-25" was applied to his buttocks with an oxwhip in front of the 40,000 inmates. The prisoners had to count the strokes audibly; if he was unable to speak, the counting began from the start. Then his open wounds were treated with iodine, and he was ordered to do several deep kneebends to prove himself still fit.

More clandestine punishment occurred, especially to secure information, in the camp showers where the prisoners bathed and were deloused once a month. A guard wired the prisoner's thumbs behind his back and threw the end of the wire over the shower pipes, raising the prisoner off his feet and letting him dangle in agony until he supplied the needed answers.

But the haunting fear was of falling ill — with diarrhea, enteritis, edema, and especially typhus, which raged through the camp the two final winters, then 200-300 died each day. Only one sign in the camp told the truth: "One louse means death." Each night the prisoners carefully deloused their clothing, finding sometimes 100 vermin. But often they were simply too exhausted, and they ended in the dreaded infirmary, burning with thirst and screaming with fever. When the SS refused to enter the contagious wards, 20 priests volunteered, bathing the victims' bodies with lysol and stacking their bodies in the alleys, like cordwood.

Several barracks served as laboratories for medical experiments. Dr. Klaus Schilling injected inmates with malaria, tuberculosis, and pus to study the effects of various drugs — or no drugs. His favorite subjects were Polish priests and seminarians between the ages of 20 and 45 — at least 140 of them had their death certificates completed before the experiments even began.

Dr. Sigmund Rascher locked prisoners into tanks from which all the oxygen was slowly withdrawn, to study methods of aiding Luftwaffe airmen whose pressurized cabins were damaged at high altitudes. Other inmates were covered with ice and once an hour sluiced with cold water to test methods of reviving airmen downed in the North Sea.

Despite the starvation, the dawn-to-dusk workdays and the harassment, these men managed to wangle a dormitory as a chapel which they slowly adorned with bits and pieces liberated from here and there in a form of "occult compensation": vestments, draperies, a monstrance made from empty fish cans. When Bishop Gabriel Piguet of Clermont-Ferrand was imprisoned in Dachau, the priests succeeded in ordaining a young German seminarian, Karl Leisner, who was dying of tuberculosis — with full vestments, biretta, miter, a crozier and ring for the bishop, made in the Messerschmidt factory — and the SS never found out.

Communion radiated out through the camp in aspirin tins and cigarette packets. Priests heard the confessions of workers who squatted next to them weeding on the plantation.

Every night at the wire surrounding the priests' barracks, starving prisoners whined the names of priests they knew could be counted on for a bit of bread. When two priests got jobs in the package depot, they distributed parcels to the worst cases, especially to the Russians.

Former university professors set up classes in theology for seminarians. Each year the priests made an eight-day retreat — the points for meditation typed and mimeographed in the job office; every Sunday evening, a seminar: the Church after the war, the human development of the priest, adaptation of the apostolate to the real life from which their priestly position had so long insulated them but which they now so painfully had rediscovered.

Perhaps there is a reason the lives and deaths of these quite surely saintly men should exclude them as authentic victims of the Holocaust.

But if the Holocaust taught us anything, it surely taught us the idiocy of inflexible dividing lines: nationalism, denominationalism, racism, sexism. Of course our ethnic, national, religious traditions are a source of rootedness, identity, and community. But not when it ceases to be a matter of honest pride and corrodes into divisiveness and bitterness.

There is only one race: the human race. All other divisions must yield to that all-inclusive un-division. At the first Christmas, their was room in the stable, so the legend goes, for Jewish shepherds and for three kings — one white, one black, one yellow. The Holocaust was an affront not merely to Jews, or to Slavs, but to the one race we all share, In the Kingdom of the one Father we also share, there are many mansions. Some are crowned with stars, others with crosses. But He dwells within them all.

The
Christmas
Editorials

Appendix C

The Christmas Editorials

On Christmas Day, 1941, the *New York Times,* commenting on Pius XII's Christmas Message, carried the following editorial:

The Pope's Message
The voice of Pius XII is a lonely voice in the silence and darkness enveloping Europe this Christmas. The Pope reiterates what he has said before. In general, he repeats, although with greater definiteness, the five-point plan for peace which he first enunciated in his Christmas message after the war broke out in 1939. His program agrees in fundamentals with the Roosevelt-Churchill eight-point declaration. It calls for respect for treaties and the end of the possibility of aggression, equal treatment for minorities, freedom from religious persecution. It goes farther than the Atlantic Charter in advocating an end of all national monopolies of economic wealth, and not so far as the eight points, which

demands complete disarmament for Germany pending some future limitation of arms for all nations.

The Pontiff emphasized principles of international morality with which most men of good-will agree. He uttered the ideas a spiritual leader would be expected to express in time of war. Yet his words sound strange and bold in the Europe of today, and we comprehend the complete submergence and enslavement of great nations, the very sources of our civilization, as we realize that he is about the only ruler left on the Continent of Europe who dares to raise his voice at all. The last tiny islands of neutrality are so hem-med in and over-shadowed by war and fear that no one but the Pope is still able to speak aloud in the name of the Prince of Peace. This is indeed a measure of the "moral devastation" he describes as the accompaniment of physical ruin and inconceivable human suffering.

In calling for a "real new order" based on "liberty, justice and love," to be attained only by a "return to social and international principles capable of creating a barrier against the abuse of liberty and the abuse of power," the Pope put himself squarely against Hitlerism. Recognizing that there is no road open to agreement between belligerents "whose reciprocal war aims and programs seem to be irreconcilable," he left no doubt that the Nazi aims are also irreconcilable with his own conception of a Christian peace. "The new order which must arise out of this war," he asserted, "must be based on principles." And that implies only one end to the war.

On Christmas Day, 1942, the *Times* once again editorialized on the papal Christmas Message and again praised Pius XII for his moral leadership:

The Pope's Verdict

No Christmas sermon reaches a larger congregation than the message Pope Pius XII addresses to a war-torn world at this season. This Christmas more than ever he is a lonely voice crying out of the silence of a continent. The Pulpit whence he speaks is more than ever like the Rock on which the Church was founded, a tiny island lashed and surrounded by a sea of war. In these circumstances, in any circumstances, indeed, no one would expect the Pope to speak as a political leader, or a war leader, or in any other role than that of a preacher ordained to stand above the battle, tied impartially, as he says, to all people and willing to collaborate in any new order which will bring a just peace.

But just because the Pope speaks to and in some sense for all the peoples at war, the clear stand he takes on the fundamental issues of the conflict has greater weight and authority. When a leader bound impartially to nations on both sides condemns as heresy the new form of national state which subordinates everything to itself: when he declares that whoever wants peace must protect against "arbitrary attacks" the "juridical safety of individuals:" when he assails violent occupation of territory, the exile and persecution of human beings for no reason other than race or political opinion: when he says that people must fight for a just and decent peace, a "total peace" — the "impartial judgment" is like a verdict in a high court of justice.

Pope Pius expresses as passionately as any leader on our side the war aims of the struggle for freedom when he says that those who aim at building a new world must fight for free choice of government and religious order. They must refuse that the state should make of individuals a herd of whom the state disposes as if they were lifeless thing.